PATH TO BUDDHAHOOD

PATH TO
ƁUDDHAHOOD

TEACHINGS ON GAMPOPA'S
Jewel Ornament of Liberation

Ringu Tulku

Foreword by Matthieu Ricard

Edited by Briona Nic Dhiarmada,
Maggy Jones, and Corinne Segers

Shambhala
Boston & London · 2003

Shambhala Publications, Inc.
Horticultural Hall
300 Massachusetts Avenue
Boston, Massachusetts 02115
www.shambhala.com

Originally published in French under the title
Et si vous m'expliquiez le bouddhisme?
©2001 NiL Editions, Paris

Translation ©2003 NiL Editions, Paris

9 8 7 6 5 4 3 2 1

First Edition
Printed in the United States of America

♾ This edition is printed on acid-free paper that meets the
American National Standards Institute Z39.48 Standard.
Distributed in the United States by Random House, Inc.,
and in Canada by Random House of Canada Ltd

Library of Congress Cataloging-in-Publication Data
Ringu Tulku.
    Path to Buddhahood: teachings on Gampopa's jewel ornament of
liberation/Ringu Tulku Rinpoche; Edited by Maggy Jones, Briona Nic
Dhiarmada, and Corinne Segers.
    p.   cm.
Includes index.
ISBN 1-59030-012-2 (pbk. : alk. paper)
1. Sgam-po-pa, 1079–1153 Dam chos yid bâzin gyi nor bu thar pa rin po
che i rgyan.   2. Bodhisattva stages (Mahayana Buddhism)—Early works to
1800.   3. Mahayana Buddhism—Doctrines—Early works to 1800.
4. Religious life—Mahayana Buddhism—Early works to 1800.   I. Jones,
Maggy.   II. Dhiarmada, Briona Nic.   III. Segers, Corinne.   IV. Title.
BQ4330.R56 2003
294.3'42—dc21
2003003850

All my chatter in the name of Dharma has been set down faithfully by my dear students of pure vision. I pray that at least a fraction of the wisdom of those enlightened teachers who tirelessly trained me may shine through the mass of my incoherence.

May this help to dispel the darkness of unknowing in the minds of all beings and lead them to complete realization, free from all fear.

CONTENTS

FOREWORD

Path to Buddhahood constitutes one of the best introductions to the teachings of Tibetan Buddhism available today. In simple, intelligent language, using images that appeal to our everyday experience and yet are surprisingly subtle, Ringu Tulku Rinpoche guides us with clarity to the discovery of the basic principles of the contemplative and philosophical path of Buddhism as it is practiced in Tibet.

Here he both extracts the quintessence from and gives a commentary on *The Jewel Ornament of Liberation*, a text composed by Gampopa, the main spiritual son of the great hermit Milarepa.

In the genre known as the gradual path, Gampopa's manual is a classic that guides us step by step toward enlightenment. The stages of this path are in no way artificial: they mark the unfolding of the inner transformation, of the growth that makes a spiritual child an adult in wisdom. To try to hurry the process in an artificial way risks withering the bud of knowledge before it can even bloom. It is therefore of the highest importance that a practitioner become familiar with each of these stages and practice them until obtaining a real inner experience. The Tibetan yogi Shabkar warns us against impatience, which could make us neglect this essential aspect of the path and wish to arrive at the destination without even having traveled:

> In our times, certain people say, "It's not necessary to use so much effort to accomplish the preliminary practices. Why complicate life? It's enough to just practice mahamudra, which transcends all concept." But that's the same as saying, "Although I can't chew butter, I'm going to chew stones." Don't listen to such nonsense. How can someone arrive at the ocean who has not crossed over land?[1]

The teaching of Ringu Tulku Rinpoche shows us the value and the meaning of human life, the significance of death and of impermanence, the law of karma and the sufferings inherent in the world of conditions, samsara. It extols the virtues of renunciation, the necessity of following a qualified master and putting his or her teachings into practice. It shows us that compassion is the main characteristic of an authentic practitioner, compassion that has us wish: "Until enlightenment, I will do everything in my power to help others, without omitting a single being, friend, enemy, or stranger." It is said:

Who has compassion possesses all the teachings;
Who does not have it possesses none of them.

Compassion teaches us the essence of generosity: the nonattachment that endures adversity and triumphs over outbursts of anger; the diligence through which one binds oneself to the practice without distraction by eliminating all laziness; the concentration that dominates obscuring emotions and discursive thoughts; and finally, the wisdom that unveils the ultimate nature of phenomena, the understanding of emptiness intimately tied to a boundless compassion, the realization of buddha nature within each being, the primordial, unchangeable purity of all phenomena.

The lucid explanations of Ringu Tulku provide us with the indispensable basis of a spiritual practice that allies knowledge and experience, rigor and inspiration.

Matthieu Ricard

PREFACE

THE TEXT

The *Dagpo Tarjen*[1] or *The Jewel Ornament of Liberation*[2] of Gampopa is one of the most important texts of Tibetan Buddhism. In the Kagyu[3] tradition it is the main text used in the instruction of monks. It is sometimes referred to as the "merging of the two streams" because Gampopa here combines two traditions or currents of Dharma teachings, that of the Mahayana Kadampa[4] tradition and that of the tantric Mahamudra[5] tradition.

Gampopa's teachings brought these two traditions together in such a way that they could be practiced together as one experience. They quickly became one of the most important and effective foundation texts used in the teaching of Buddhism in Tibet from the eleventh century onward. The whole Kagyu tradition is based mainly on this teaching.

THE AUTHOR

Gampopa was born in 1079 and died in 1153. Despite his renown as a physician, he was unable to save his wife and two children, who died in an epidemic that ravaged the region where they lived. Full of grief, he came to a deep understanding of the transitory nature of all things and the inherent suffering that this implied. He renounced the world and devoted himself totally to spiritual practice, seeking a way out of the suffering of samsara. Gampopa became a monk and for many years followed the teachings of the Kadampa *geshes*[6] of the time. One day he happened to hear the name of Milarepa, the famous Tibetan yogic poet, and intense devotion immediately arose in him. Deeply inspired, he began to cry and left at once to seek out Milarepa.

After many hardships Gampopa arrived near the place where the yogi was staying. Having traveled without any rest, Gampopa was by now ill and exhausted. The people in the local village took him in and treated him with great respect and hospitality. "You must be the one whom Milarepa spoke of," they said. "What did he say about me?" asked Gampopa. The villagers replied that Milarepa had predicted his arrival, telling them, "A monk from Ü[7] is coming. He is a very great bodhisattva and will be the holder of my lineage. Whoever shows him hospitality when he first arrives will be liberated from samsara and will enjoy the best of good fortune."

When Gampopa heard this, he said to himself, "I must be a very special person." Feelings of pride and conceit arose in his mind, and, consequently, when he went to meet Milarepa in his cave, the latter refused to see him. He had Gampopa wait in a nearby cave for fifteen days. When he was finally allowed to see Milarepa, Gampopa found the yogi sitting there with a skull cup full of wine. He handed the skull to Gampopa and invited him to drink. Gampopa was perplexed. He was a fully ordained monk and as such had vowed to abstain from alcohol. Yet here was Milarepa commanding him to drink. It was unthinkable! So great, however, was Gampopa's trust and devotion to his guru that he took the skull cup and drained it of every drop.

This act had a very nice and auspicious significance, as it showed that Gampopa was completely open and ready to receive the entirety of Milarepa's teachings and full realization. It is said that how much a student can benefit from a teacher depends upon how open he or she is. Although Gampopa was a very good monk, he drank the skull cup of wine without any hesitation or reservation, which signified that he was completely open and without the slightest doubt.

Milarepa subsequently gave Gampopa his complete teachings, and within a very short time Gampopa became his best and most realized student.[8] In Gampopa's teachings we therefore find the scholarly erudition and discipline of his monastic tradition combined with the total realization of a fully accomplished yogi, which he received through Milarepa.

The present commentary relies mainly on the original Tibetan text but draws upon both Guenther's and Holmes's translations where necessary.

ACKNOWLEDGMENTS

This book was put together from a series of teachings that I gave on Gampopa's *Jewel Ornament of Liberation* at Samye Dzong, in Brussels, in 1993 and 1994. It is not really meant to be a commentary, but more of an introduction to that great classic. I would very much like to thank the staff of Samye Dzong, as well as the participants of those programs, as their questions and our ensuing discussions made the subject more relevant to our times.

Special thanks go to those students who transcribed and edited the manuscript and made the publication of this book possible: Maria Huendorf-Kaiser; Maggy Jones; and Briona Nic Dhiarmada and her group—Pat Little, Loan McDermott, Chloe Jenner, and Emile and Alison Lopez—and Corinne Segers.

This book would not have come into being without the support of Matthieu Ricard, who not only wrote the foreword and presented the manuscript to its French publisher, NiL, but also revised the French manuscript, which served as the basis for this English edition. I owe my deepest gratitude to him.

My thanks also go to Sam Bercholz and Emily Bower of Shambhala Publications for their support and final editing, respectively.

Many other people contributed in various ways to the successful completion of this book and, although I don't have the space to mention all their names here, I would like to extend my heartfelt thanks to them all for their precious help.

Finally, I would like to express my deepest gratitude to my masters. If you find anything useful in this book, it comes from them.

HOMAGE TO MANJUSHRI

As is the tradition in all Tibetan and Sanskrit texts, *The Jewel Ornament of Liberation* begins with the homage, in this case an homage to Manjushri.[9]

The homage is considered to be a very important element in the text. It is said that a superior student, one with supreme intelligence, needs only to hear the title of a text to fully understand its content. For a student of the next level, one with a very great intelligence, it is enough to hear the homage. It is also said that if the teacher is wise and intelligent enough, he can teach the whole text from simply describing the title and the homage.

The homage begins:

I prostrate to Manjushri, the ever-young. I pay homage with profound respect to the buddhas, bodhisattvas, and all the noble dharmas[10] and to the gurus who are the true root of them all.

A bodhisattva is anyone, man or woman, who decides to work toward becoming an enlightened being, a buddha, for the benefit of others. Anyone who thinks and works in this way, no matter what religion he or she follows, if any, is a bodhisattva.

Bodhisattvas are sometimes referred to as the sons[11] and sometimes as the fathers of the buddhas. The relationship of a bodhisattva to a buddha is similar to that of a prince to a king. Once you become a bodhisattva, sooner or later you are certain to become a buddha in the same way a hereditary prince or princess becomes a king or queen. However, in order to become a buddha, one first has to become a bodhisattva. From this angle, bodhisattvas "produce" buddhas. This is why they are also sometimes called fathers or parents of the buddhas.

Gampopa continues by paying homage to "all the noble Dharmas." This means that, according to Buddhism, there is not one Dharma, not one teaching, not one right way. There are many hundreds and thousands of them. A path is good if it leads one in the right direction. Because there are so many different types of people, each with his or her own needs, one path could not suit everybody. A variety of ways are needed, which is why there are many Dharmas.

Gampopa also pays homage to the root of all Dharmas: the lama,[12] or guru. The lama is the one who gives us the teachings, who explains to us the meaning of, for example, buddhas, bodhisattvas, enlightenment, the Dharma, and so on. In Tibet, the title "root lama"[13] was given to the lama from whom one received the most profound teachings and through whom one recognized the nature of mind.

The homage finishes:

By the grace of the blessings and the kindness of Milarepa, I now write this jewel-like noble Dharma, which is like the wish-fulfilling gem, for my own benefit and the benefit of all others.

Milarepa, of course, was Gampopa's lama. Gampopa is telling us here that it is thanks to Milarepa that the knowledge he received through his lama's blessing is being passed on to us through his writing.

This then is the meaning of the homage. We are now ready to begin the text proper.

INTRODUCTION

From a Buddhist perspective, all phenomena can be categorized as being in samsara or nirvana. That is to say, all of us, all beings, are either in the state of samsara or nirvana—there is nothing outside of these. Samsara describes our present state of existence, in which we are not free from suffering. Nirvana is the state of enlightenment, when we see everything as it truly is. It is the state of buddhahood. When one has complete realization, one is in nirvana. If not, one is in samsara. Gampopa begins his text by giving us a description of the essential characteristics of these two states.

THE NATURE OF SAMSARA

He makes three points about samsara: "Its ultimate nature is shunyata (emptiness), its appearance (the form it takes) is confusion, and its primary characteristic is suffering."

1. Shunyata

In Buddhism, everything is considered to be *shunyata*, or emptiness, in its essence, whether it is nirvana or samsara. The term *shunyata* is notoriously difficult to translate or to define. It is usually rendered as "emptiness" or "void." Although I am using the word "emptiness" here, I use it with some reservation. It is important to understand that although the word *shunya* in Sanskrit means "empty," to say as Gampopa does that phenomena are empty by their nature does not mean that they are empty in the sense that they do not exist. That is not what is meant here. "Interdependence" would perhaps be a better term to use, as it signifies that everything exists because of something else and depends upon something else. Because everything is interdependent, nothing can be said to exist separately, in and of itself. Without the sun, for example, there would be no trees; without trees, this book could not exist. As all phenomena can be shown to be interrelated in this way, we can therefore say that all phenomena are empty of an essential independent nature. This is what is meant by the philosophical view of shunyata. It is discussed in chapter 4 in more detail.

2. Confusion

Having stated that the nature of samsara is emptiness, shunyata, Gampopa goes on to say that "its appearance is confusion," or *trulwa*.[14] This means that the manifestation of samsara is a mistaken perception of reality. This term *trulwa* is a highly significant one in Buddhist philosophy. It means literally "hallucination," seeing something not as it truly is. Samsara is confusion, a wrong way of seeing, a misconception, an illusion. From the Buddhist point of view it is trulwa. This mistaken perception, this misconception, this illusion, this confusion is the root of all our unhappiness and all our suffering.

3. Suffering

The third characteristic of samsara is suffering. If we experience suffering, this automatically implies that we are in samsara. If we don't have this mistaken perception, then we don't have suffering and we are no longer in samsara. The absence or presence of confusion and its consequent suffering is the main difference between samsara and nirvana.

THE NATURE OF NIRVANA

Gampopa also makes three points about nirvana.

1. Shunyata

Like samsara, its nature is emptiness (shunyata).

2. Exhaustion of Confusion

Unlike samsara, its appearance or manifestation is the complete cessation, the complete exhaustion of all the confusion, all the mistaken perception.

3. Liberation from Suffering

Its characteristic is liberation from all kinds of sufferings. So the basic principle is very simple. We just need to see the true nature of ourselves and of phenomena and we are liberated from samsara and suffering.

THE NATURE OF SUFFERING

In Buddhist cosmology, beings are categorized as belonging to six classes, or six realms,[15] as they are traditionally known. Every sentient being belongs to one of these classes and experiences the type of suffering and confusion particular to that realm.

Whether they inhabit the higher or the lower realms, all beings live under the influence of confusion and mistaken perceptions. Every being who suffers, or who is capable of suffering, or who simply possesses the causes for suffering, lives in samsara.

We might wonder what is the source, the basis, of these mistaken perceptions and the sufferings that ensue? Gampopa answers that there is no basis as such. All the sufferings are by nature empty (shunyata) and therefore baseless, but they have a cause, and that cause is ignorance.[16] "Ignorance" here does not mean a lack of knowledge or a lack of information. What is meant here is a lack of comprehension, a lack of understanding of the true nature of things. And the true nature of things is that they are empty.

This confusion is similar to a dream. When we are sleeping and we start to dream, our dream experiences seem very real. We can feel them, we can sense them, we believe it's all truly happening, but when we wake up, we realize that nothing has actually happened. In reality, we were just lying comfortably in bed.

In the same way, all samsara is like a dream. It is important to understand that we are not saying here that it is a dream but that it is similar to a dream. When we wake up from samsara, we realize that nothing was actually happening, just like in a dream.

All the suffering, all the happiness, everything that we experience now seems very real to us. When we become enlightened, when we awaken from samsara, we realize that all our experiences, all our emotions were in reality manifestations without any substantial reality, without any intrinsic existence—just like dreams. Therefore, we say that samsara has no beginning, but it does have an end. When we are dreaming, we have no sense of a beginning of the dream, nor any idea that now we are in the middle of the dream—we are simply in the dream. We do know, however, when the dream ends because that's when we wake up.

Many people wonder when sentient beings have entered samsara and how they could ever do so if they all have the buddha nature, the seed of buddhahood within themselves. This is a very difficult question, because there is no answer as long as our reasoning is still based on the premise of a substantial, truly existing reality. What is important to remember is that samsara is founded on a mistaken perception and therefore on an illusion. Gampopa tells us that, as it's an illusion, we cannot say that it has any beginning, since it doesn't exist in the way ordinary beings perceive it in the first place.

The question is also often asked as to why living in samsara should constitute a problem. Even if it is an illusion, even if it is only a dream, it may still be a nice dream, so why should it matter? We don't suffer all the time. Sometimes our lives can appear to be very happy. But the Buddha tells us that if we look into it more deeply, we will see that even when we seem not to be suffering, when we are apparently very happy, we are actually suffering, although without being conscious of it. As we are in samsara, suffering is always latent in whatever we do or whatever we are. Even when we are happy, we fear that things might change, that our happiness will not last. For example, a simple knock on the door or a telephone call late at night can lead to worry or fear. We know that things cannot last, and we fear the change. This is the suffering or unease inherent in samsara. As long as we are in samsara, there is no complete peace. This is why Gampopa tells us that fundamentally samsara is suffering.

We can then wonder whether this suffering can go away on its own. Gampopa answers that there is no possibility that this confusion will disappear by itself. Samsara is confusion by definition, and confusion automatically leads to suffering, which gives rise to more confusion and still more suffering. Therefore, it will not go away by itself. We need to do something about it, and Gampopa advises us to do all we can to get out of samsara and try to attain the realization of nirvana.

THE SIX FACTORS

To achieve this goal, Gampopa explains that six factors are necessary:

1. The cause,
2. The basis,

3. The condition,
4. The method,
5. The result, and
6. The activity.

These six factors are the topic of Gampopa's book and are delineated in the following chapters.

1. THE CAUSE:

Buddha Nature

The first factor is the *ju,*[1] which translates literally as "cause." In this context, it has three meanings: primary cause, seed, and nature. This is the buddha nature that is inherent in everyone. It is what gives us the possibility of getting out of samsara and attaining enlightenment, or nirvana. We should, however, understand that this is just a way of speaking.

Samsara and nirvana are not two separate places or locations: one does not leave the one to enter the other. This is one of the most important and basic principles of Buddhism. Once in nirvana, one never returns to samsara, because nirvana is not some destination to be reached but an understanding of the true nature of samsara. It is a permanent state, because it means understanding and total wisdom. What we call samsara is our state of confusion and suffering. To understand the true nature of the suffering implies an understanding of how things truly are. As the confusion disappears, so does the suffering.

That is nirvana. As is said in the beginning, the basic nature of samsara and nirvana are the same: they are both what we call shunyata, or emptiness.

BUDDHA NATURE

The seed refers to our buddha nature. We can attain enlightenment because we already possess the nature of a buddha. All living beings have this buddha nature. One might wonder how we know this. Traditionally we are presented with three distinct types of evidence.

The first is scriptural authority. Buddha Shakyamuni himself asserted the presence of buddha nature, and we have every reason to trust what he said, as he himself attained buddhahood. Who better to tell us whether buddha nature exists or not? In the *Samadhiraja Sutra,*[2] the Buddha says, "The essence of buddhahood[3] pervades all beings." Likewise, the *Mahaparinirvana Sutra* says, "All beings possess the nature of buddha, or tathagatagarbha." This same sutra goes on to explain that buddha nature is inherent in all beings, as butter is inherent in milk. This assertion was made not only by Buddha himself but also by his successors, particularly those who founded and developed Mahayana Buddhism such as Asanga and Nagarjuna.

The second way to demonstrate the existence of buddha nature consists rather in describing precisely what buddha nature is and then determining if and how it manifests in beings. The nature of both samsara and nirvana is shunyata. Therefore, the basic nature of all beings is also shunyata. This is synonymous with the term *dharmakaya*. In Buddhism there is much talk of the "three *kayas*": dharmakaya, *sambhogakaya,* and *nirmanakaya*. These ideas are not the most easily accessible at first, but they will be explained in more details in later chapters. *Dharmakaya* has many different meanings, but here I use the term to describe the true, ultimate nature of phenomena. In this context the word *dharma* signifies "true appearance" or "true nature," while *kaya* means "form." *Dharmakaya* means therefore "the form of the true nature or ultimate reality." Whether one is in samsara or nirvana, our true nature can be nothing other than this ultimate truth, or *dharmakaya*. If we understand, experience, and realize this ultimate nature, this fundamental truth, we attain—indeed we become—the dharmakaya. The true nature, the dharmakaya, does not change. Nothing has ever altered it. Whether one is a samsaric being or an enlightened being, the dharmakaya isn't any smaller or worse in the former or any bigger or better in the latter. A buddha and an ordinary being have exactly the same basic nature. Attaining buddhahood does not mean we become someone completely different. Rather we become fully conscious of what we have always been. It isn't something that "descends upon us," but rather is an understanding, a realization. Our confusion disappears. We can compare samsara to a thick fog that prevents us from seeing anything except as vague and confused shapes. When the mist clears, the landscape hasn't changed, but now we see it clearly.

Finally, although we are in samsara, we can still see the proof of the existence of buddha nature permeating all living beings. This third way in which we can discern whether beings have buddha nature is *rig*,[4] in other words, the quality we perceive in one who possesses this buddha nature. *Rig* is a word that is difficult to translate. Literally, it means "caste." Guenther translates it as "family," but it is not quite that. It means something more like a "tribal gene." For example, Europeans often have fair hair and blue eyes. Orientals have black hair and eyes. This is due to *rig*. All beings have buddha nature because all beings have within themselves what we call the essence of the buddha, this *ju*, this seed, which can blossom into a buddha and which constitutes our potential for enlightenment.

But what is a buddha? Briefly, a buddha is one who has developed his or her compassion and wisdom to the ultimate level, beyond all limits. Wisdom, in this context, refers not to an accumulation of knowledge but to the ability to see the true nature of all things. What characterizes a buddha therefore is wisdom and compassion.

To determine whether buddha nature exists in all beings, we need to examine whether they possess the qualities of wisdom and compassion. Without wisdom and compassion, it is impossible to become a buddha, but if one possesses even an embryonic amount of these qualities, one can then develop them to their ultimate level and become buddha. The most concrete proof of the presence of this nature is that we possess, to varying degrees, these qualities of wisdom and compassion.

According to Buddhism, there is no being, human or otherwise, who doesn't possess some wisdom and compassion. However bad, however evil, every being has some minimal amount of love, kindness, or compassion, at least for themselves or for one other being. Similarly, all of us have some understanding, instinctual or otherwise, of what is right or wrong. These two qualities, kindness and the understanding of right from wrong, however small or insignificant they are, are present in every living being. As these two qualities can potentially be developed to their ultimate level, it can be said that all beings have buddha nature. We can therefore all be said to be "little buddhas"!

THE FIVE STAGES

Gampopa goes on to describe how the rig, or the qualities visible in buddha nature, develop in five stages.

The first stage is called *rig che*,[5] which literally means "cut off from the caste or family" and describes the state of those whose buddha nature is not apparent. They can be recognized by six signs: They feel no sorrow in the face of the shortcomings of samsara and no desire for liberation. Even when they experience intense suffering, they don't recognize the causes. They don't even see that there is a problem. They feel no confidence or trust when they hear about the qualities of the buddhas and the states superior to samsara. They feel no culpability when they harm others. The whole world can criticize them, but they feel no shame. They never feel the slightest remorse nor the slightest compassion. The beings who present these signs belong to the family of those with "switched-off" potential. They appear not to have the required qualities, and they live as if they didn't possess buddha nature. This does not mean, however, that they will never become buddhas, but it does mean that it will take them a long time.

The second stage groups those whose situation is not definite. Their buddha nature manifests according to the circumstances. When they are under a good influence or in a good frame of mind, then their buddha nature can be seen. When the same people are in a bad mood or in bad company, then they show no compassion or kindness and their buddha nature seems to disappear.

The third stage is that of the *shravakas*. They recognize that samsara offers nothing but problems and unhappiness and have resolved to leave it all behind. They tend to focus their efforts on attaining nirvana by concentrating on developing their wisdom but not their compassion.

The fourth stage is that of the *pratyekabuddhas*. They have the same qualities as the shravakas. They are very intelligent but also very proud and arrogant. They give no credit to their teachers and wish to find their own path. Even if they do have a guide, or if somebody gives them good advice, their pride won't let them admit it because they want to advance by themselves. For them Buddha has taught what is called the shravaka and pratyekabuddha path, which leads to the state of *arhat*. An arhat is liberated from the sufferings of samsara but is not yet ready to become a buddha. Arhats are sort of "foe destroyers" who destroy their enemies, not external but inner enemies, their own negative emotions. Having eliminated their negative emotions, they no longer experience any unhappiness, because suffering arises out of negative emotions. Nevertheless, they still have some progress to make in order to become fully realized beings.

The fifth and highest stage is that of the bodhisattvas. Here we can distinguish two different aspects regarding the potential of bodhisattvas: the potential that exists naturally and the potential that is acquired. We are referring here to the potential already inherent in all beings to become bodhisattvas and the potential they have to develop the qualities leading to enlightenment. This potential is realized in those who have engaged in virtuous actions in the course of their past lives. When we speak about the "family of bodhisattvas," we are usually referring to this category. We can say that those in whom the qualities of wisdom and compassion are apparent belong to this family of bodhisattvas.

According to Gampopa, there are two types of bodhisattvas: those who are "evolved" thanks to their positive actions and efforts in previous lives, in whom the characteristics are apparent, and those who are not, in whom the characteristics are latent. The latter have all the qualities of a bodhisattva but still remain under the influence of hindrances and negative emotions. These hindrances or obstacles can, however, be overcome if the person concerned works at it. Whatever the case, the characteristics of a bodhisattva can be more visible at certain times than at others.

In the *Dashadharmaka Sutra*, it says: "The potential of bodhisattvas is detected by its signs, as fire is recognized through smoke and water detected by the presence of waterfowl." We might wonder what these signs are. The body and speech of bodhisattvas are by nature gentle, regardless of the influence of a spiritual friend. Their mind and character are not tainted by fraud or deceit, and they feel love for all beings. There is also a great inner purity. Therefore, if someone, without coming under the positive influence of someone else, is naturally kind, full of compassion, and without duplicity, then he or she is a member of the family of bodhisattvas and is very near to becoming or developing into a buddha.

All living beings have these qualities latent within them. Through work and practice, all of us can succeed in developing into and becoming buddhas. There is no reason to think that the sufferings of samsara are inevitable or that we have to accept them as such. If we are suffering, we can do something about it. All our sufferings, all our neuroses, are merely temporary and can be totally eliminated. Even when we are in the grip of confusion and undergoing great sufferings, there is no need to fall prey to frustration and despair: there is hope! It is not necessary to wait until the next life to change from one "family" or stage to another. In Buddhist philosophy, this life is not some static state in which we live before passing on to the next. Moving from this life to the next is simply one change in the midst of constant changes. What we call the next life then is merely a continuation of this process of change. Change is possible every single second, since change occurs every single second. It is not necessary to wait until the next life in order to transform oneself. Indeed, if we don't decide to take full responsibility for improving our future lives, there is often very little change as to our general status from one life to the next. According to Buddhism, what we do now creates the following moment, which creates the one after that. In the same way, the moment of our death creates the next moment, which in this case is our next life.

2. THE BASIS:

A Precious Human Life

The second of the six conditions for reaching enlightenment is *ten*,[1] which Guenther translates as "the working basis." This is, in effect, what we call in Tibetan *mi lu rin chen*:[2] our precious human body.

Although all beings have buddha nature, certain forms of existence are not conducive to its development or realization. Although theoretically it is possible to become enlightened in any form of existence, the easiest and best circumstance in which to attain our ultimate goal is as a human being. If, as well as having human form, we have five extra qualities, we can then be said to have a *precious human body*. Two of these five conditions refer to the body and three to the mind.

The first right condition for the body is what we call the eight freedoms. These freedoms enable one to develop a leisurely approach to life. A quotation from a sutra lists the eight states that are the opposite of the eight right conditions of freedom or leisure. The first is the condition of the hell beings. The second is that of the hungry ghosts. The third is the condition of animals. The fourth is that of the gods. The fifth state is that of barbarians, who have no awareness of the Dharma. The sixth is the state of the beings who harbor completely wrong views. The seventh is the condition of beings living where there has never been any buddha. The eighth is a state of total stupidity, of being unable to understand anything. A being who lives in any of these eight states has no opportunity to practice Dharma because the conditions are not right. Indeed, if you are in one of these states you are either too preoccupied with your own unhappiness or too busy trying to enjoy yourself to have any opportunity or motivation to practice Dharma. If you are a hell being or a hungry ghost or a similar being, you experience so much misery and despair that you have no time to practice, or no intention to, or really no thought at all of Dharma. If you are in a very good realm, like the god realm, it is said that you have no time then either, because you spend all your time enjoying yourself! Since you do not notice anything wrong, since there's no misery or suffering around, you have no motivation to do anything except seek pleasure.

This is why it is said that the human realm, the human existence, is the perfect condition for the practice of Dharma. In this human body we know about unhappiness, but we also have some leisure time. We are not completely controlled by our own conditionings; we have some freedom of will. At the same time, we see the problems of others, their troubles and their unhappiness, which gives us the opportunity to develop compassion and the motivation to work steadily toward the solution to these problems.

Certain texts and certain people maintain that there really are places like the hell realms and the god realm and that you physically go to these places. However, in the *Bodhicharyavatara*, Shantideva asks, "The burning grounds of the hells, the guards of the hell realm, who made them?" Nobody made them. These places come out of our own negative thoughts or negative emotions. These realms are not physical places that we can go to. They exist only in our mind, and we can only find them through our own mind. For instance, if we really hate something and if we die with this hatred and violence still in our mind, it is said that we could be born into the hell realm. But the hell realm will be our own creation. The hell realm could be in this place or that, at the same time; it could be anywhere or everywhere because it is in our own mind. The human realm feels as though it is really there, but there is no difference between the hell realm, the human realm, the spirit realm, or the heavenly realm. All of them are of the same nature. The human realm is no more "real" than the hell realm, and the hell realm is no less "real" than the human realm. All of them are of the same nature. They are as real as our experience of them, and these experiences come mostly from our own mind, with, of course, many different causes and effects, but through our own karma.

The second right condition for the body is what are called the ten great possessions, or the ten great riches. These are divided into two parts: the first five are innate, and the second five are those that we can only acquire thanks to others. The first five innate or personal conditions are:

1. To be born as a human being;
2. To be born in a "central" place, a place where there is the opportunity to learn and understand what is right and wrong, where people are not compelled to live under someone else's power and given no freedom, where both the Dharma and the freedom to practice prevail;
3. Not to be completely disabled, unable to understand anything or to communicate;
4. To have the understanding of what is right and what is wrong; and
5. To have a right livelihood, not to earn one's living by totally negative means, such as making weapons of war or poisoning people with bad food.

The five great possessions that come through other people are:

1. That a buddha appeared in this world,
2. That the buddha gave his teachings,

3. That these teachings are still alive,
4. That there are still people following those teachings, and
5. That one is in contact with these people, with dharma friends and
   teachers, who can give us these teachings.

If these ten conditions are present, then we have the ten great possessions, the ten great riches.

We already have the precious human body. Let's now think carefully and see whether we have all these ten great possessions. If we do not, let's try to create these conditions. If we do have them, then we should be happy, rejoice, and understand that, having these good conditions to practice, having this unique opportunity to end all the pain and confusion of the world and thereby help all living beings, we should work hard to achieve that goal.

It is said that obtaining a precious human body is extremely difficult. The Buddha gave this example to illustrate its rarity: Suppose a blind tortoise that lived for thousands of years at the bottom of the sea comes up to the surface once every hundred years. Suppose now there is a wooden yoke tossed about by the waves on this sea, never stopping at one place for more than a second. Is there any chance that when the tortoise comes to the surface of the water, this yoke will then sit on its neck? It is very difficult, almost impossible, but the Buddha said that this compares to the number of chances we have to obtain a precious human existence.

The great privilege of having gathered all the right conditions to practice Dharma is the direct result of merit accumulated through positive deeds. It is not by chance that we have this precious human body but because of our great efforts, our long, hard work in accumulating merit in the past. Therefore, we should not waste this very precious opportunity. If we waste it now, we may not have another for many hundreds of years.

The people who do have these right conditions are divided into three types. There are, of course, according to Buddhism, hundreds and thousands of different types of people, and each type has a different kind of approach, follows a different way, and requires a different method. All these different types of people were classified by Atisha Dipankara and other great teachers of Buddhist literature into three categories depending on their aims, their circumstances, their education, or their way of looking at life.

Those whose main objective in life is to gain a better standard of living, more worldly comfort and happiness, are regarded as the first type, the lowest level, what we call the "little personalities." They have the following understanding: "If I do good, I shall be rewarded. Therefore, in order to have a good, comfortable life, to be fortunate and rich not only now in this life but also in future ones, I must always try to behave well and accumulate positive deeds." These people do the right things, but their motivation is limited to worldly ambition.

The second type, or medium-level persons, have a slightly higher aim. They recognize that wherever they are, whatever they do, they are still in samsara and that, however good or comfortable their current situation, it can never give them complete satisfaction. Consequently, they go a little further and try to escape from samsara and cut off the roots of all unhappiness—but only out of self-interest.

The third type, the highest or greatest kind of person, not only wish to escape from their own samsaric cycle of problems and confusion but also want to help all other beings to escape as well. Their intentions, their objectives, are so huge and limitless that they are called the great beings.

Gampopa urges us to try to be this last kind. We should not merely enjoy the present comforts of the world. We should not aim merely to pull ourselves out of samsara, but we should also try to bring all other living beings to the same level of complete freedom from all suffering.

These three types of persons are categorized by the vastness of their intentions and objectives. This means that the people at the third level, the greatest personalities with the highest aims, are the nearest to becoming enlightened beings. Those with the smallest objectives are the farthest away.

These three categories are not as static as they seem to be here. They can be very fluid and changeable. Actually, I think most people first come to the Dharma to try to find the benefit of gaining some tranquillity or peace in their lives. They wish to get rid of depression, sadness, and emotional disturbances. For those people, the Dharma does bring an answer. The aim of Dharma is not just limited to that, but following the Dharma path with this basic approach will slowly lead to its higher goal. If you are looking for peace and happiness in this life, you will come to realize that it cannot be achieved completely or fully without a deeper understanding of life itself and a deeper way of dealing with emotions. One has to find a way that is not just a pinpointing of problems, or a finding of scattered solutions, one by one, but a deeper, root solution. Progressing on this path, discovering more and more about the true way of life, or the true nature of things, one goes further, one's aims and objectives slowly change—and with them one's status—and one will then find the true Dharma.

We have already discussed the two conditions of the body, and now we come to the three positive conditions of the mind. These are the three types of devotion, or the three kinds of faith.

The first is the faith of appreciation or inspiration. It springs up in the mind of someone who is impressed when he or she sees or hears something very holy or very pure. One then feels a kind of inspiration or appreciation. However, this kind of reaction is still shallow.

The second, the faith of desire, the faith of wanting, means that on seeing something very good, something inspiring, someone with great wisdom and compassion such as a buddha, a strong wish arises, "I would also like to become like that." This kind of wanting is called the faith of desire.

The third and strongest type of faith is complete trust. It is not blind faith but total confidence born from understanding. Complete understanding naturally gives rise to complete faith.

These faiths are described in more detail later, so it is not necessary to spend more time on this subject here. The important thing to notice is that, in Buddhism, when we talk about faith, we are talking mainly about understanding. Blind faith is not encouraged at all, although some people start with a blind faith, or just a feeling of inspiration. As one becomes more interested, one should study the Dharma, go deeper into it, and acquire more understanding. That way it is possible to progress from the faith of appreciation to the faith of trust. It is something that grows. Unless we have this faith of trust, we do not have complete faith. When we have complete faith we also have complete understanding. The faith of trust is described as a fundamental, most important factor, because without it we live in doubt and don't really know what we are doing.

If we have these three faiths and the right conditions of the human existence, then we have the most suitable basis for the practice of Dharma.

3. THE CONDITION:

The Spiritual Friend

The third factor, the condition[1] to reach enlightenment, is meeting a genuine spiritual friend.[2] This is a person who has the ability and willingness to guide us in the right direction and in whom we have the trust and confidence to follow.

What chains us to samsara is our deep-rooted habit of always following either the wrong direction or erroneous schemes. To help us, protect us, and encourage us to completely abandon this habit and to guide us in the right direction, we need someone strong, a friend whom we can rely upon. Without serious help, a drug addict or an alcoholic is not likely to overcome his or her addiction. In the same way, without an experienced guide whom we can totally trust, we will have a lot of difficulties getting out of the samsaric patterns to which we are deeply accustomed.

This chapter is divided into five parts. The first outlines the three reasons it is necessary to have a spiritual friend. The second lists the four categories of spiritual friend. The third describes the essential characteristics of the different types of spiritual friend. The fourth gives advice about how to enter into a relationship with a spiritual friend and specifies what questions to ask. The fifth describes the benefits that a spiritual friend brings.

WHY WE NEED A SPIRITUAL FRIEND

Gampopa justifies the need for a spiritual friend by making three points. The first is the authority of the Buddha's own words, which he quotes many times. "Good disciples devoted to their teachers should always be guided by wise and skillful mentors. Why? Because that is how their (own) qualities of skill and wisdom will emerge."[3] And again: "Thus the great bodhisattva who wishes to awaken—genuinely and totally—to peerless, utterly pure, and perfect enlightenment should from the very outset seek out, relate to, and serve good mentors."[4]

The Buddha has often repeated that the starting point of the right path is the meeting with a good spiritual friend. Indeed, one of the Three Jewels[5] is the Sangha,[6] of which spiritual friends are an integral part. They are the ones who help us, encourage us, and are the example to follow. To take refuge in the Sangha actually means that we find a good example to look up to and then we try to create an environment in which we are likely to be influenced by this model.

However, if one doesn't have too much trust in the Buddha's words, another argument is given. This second point is logically based: if we sincerely desire to stop suffering, live correctly, and realize enlightenment, there is no way to reach these goals without the help of an adequate spiritual guide. To find the right path, we must first find someone who has already treaded it. Without an appropriate guide, how can we find the path to enlightenment?

The third argument is in fact an illustration of the usefulness of a spiritual guide. Gampopa gives us several examples. If, for example, we cross the desert without a guide, we will go around in circles, lost in the immense expanse of sand. In the same way, without a skipper to cross the ocean, we will never reach the other side. We have as much need of a spiritual guide to cross the ocean of samsara and reach the shore of awakening.

A spiritual path is not just an intellectual pursuit. It is about transforming our way of experiencing and reacting to the world. We need to learn how to do that the way a musician learns how to play an instrument. We need an experienced teacher who can show us how to do that and who can help in our learning process.

THE DIFFERENT CATEGORIES OF SPIRITUAL FRIENDS

Gampopa distinguishes four categories of spiritual friends. The first groups together spiritual friends who are ordinary human beings, the second the bodhisattvas who have reached a high degree of spiritual development, the third the emanations of the buddhas in the nirmanakaya[7] form, and the fourth emanations of the buddhas in the sambhogakaya form.

Although the great bodhisattvas are ideal teachers, it's not easy for ordinary people like us to recognize a member of the latter three categories, much less make contact with one of them. The category of masters to whom ordinary people like us can have access is the first one, the masters who are not totally awakened but who are well on the way. They are more or less like us but already have a certain training, a certain level of serious spiritual practice. This type of spiritual friend is appropriate for the student of the first level.

The third category groups together the buddha's emanations. According to the scriptures of Mahayana Buddhism, Buddha Shakyamuni himself is considered a buddha emanation. He is what we call a perfect form of nirmanakaya. We can distinguish different forms of nirmanakaya or different buddha's emanation. Three types of nirmanakaya are usually mentioned: the Supreme Nirmanakaya, like Buddha Shakyamuni; manifestations by birth in human or animal form; and the "creative" manifestations, animate or inanimate (such as a bridge, a boat, or medicine). This is possible because a buddha can appear in any form that is useful and can benefit sentient beings whenever and wherever this aid is necessary.

The last category groups the real buddhas, who have realized perfect enlightenment.

Since the last three types of masters are out of reach for us, we will concentrate on the first one, the level of ordinary spiritual friends.

THE QUALITIES OF ORDINARY SPIRITUAL FRIENDS

It is very important to choose a worthy spiritual friend. This is why the qualities of a genuine teacher are clearly described.

The texts usually mention eight, four, or two qualities that are considered essential. According to a sutra called *The Bodhisattva's Levels,*[8] teachers or spiritual guides should have eight particular qualities:

1. They must first of all follow the precepts and vows of a bodhisattva.
2. They must have studied in depth the teachings of the path of the bodhisattva.
3. Their understanding must be deep and not purely intellectual; they must have truly experienced the teachings.
4. They must feel sincere compassion toward all sentient beings.
5. They must be fearless and show a lot of courage, not only in their own actions but also when they teach others.
6. They must be tolerant and patient with their students and their practice.
7. They must be tenacious and not allow themselves to be carried away by discouragement or disappointment.
8. Finally, they must be capable of communicating effectively with students.

Here's a little story illustrating why a spiritual friend should be able to communicate with his or her students properly. A monastery in Gangtok had many monks, mainly Bhutanese. The abbot invited a *khenpo* (great scholar) who was a native of the Tibetan province of

Kham to teach the monks. For two years he taught every morning and evening. It was only at the end of the second year that he realized that his students spoke a different dialect and had understood absolutely nothing of his teachings. Deeply disappointed, he dropped everything and returned to Tibet. He was an excellent teacher, but because he could not communicate with his students, he couldn't help them.

In certain other texts, the *Mahayana Sutralankara,* for example, four qualities are described. First of all, the teacher must be very learned and have vast knowledge. Next, he must have a deep analytical wisdom, which helps him conquer his students' doubts. His conduct must be perfectly virtuous and honest, so that he truly deserves the respect and confidence of everyone. Finally, he must be able to point out problems, disturbing emotions, negative aspects of life, and the means to avoid them. The teacher who has all these qualities is an authentic spiritual friend.

In the *Bodhicharyavatara,* Shantideva mentions only two qualities. First, the teacher must be well versed in the teachings related to the practices of the bodhisattvas. Second, he must practice them himself and should be ready to give up his life rather than abandon them.

THE MASTER-DISCIPLE RELATIONSHIP

Once we have found a guide who possesses all or most of the qualities previously mentioned, there are three ways in which we should behave.

First, we should show him or her our respect and try to be useful to him or her, which we can do in three ways. The first is to offer material commodities, hospitality, food, offerings, and so on. The second is to offer respect and services. The third is to offer our practice. Of the three, the last is the most valuable. The best reward a master can get for his or her efforts is to inspire students to practice and the benefits thus brought to them.

Second, to be able to practice correctly, a student must listen attentively to his or her teacher's instructions and never be afraid to ask questions. The most important thing is to eliminate doubts, to clarify whatever may seem obscure so as to practice with a clear mind. We should not be satisfied with a vague understanding or with retaining only that which suits us. Instead we should try to deepen our understanding of the teachings until no doubt or uncertainty is left. We shouldn't listen only to what we like or understand or are familiar with. This means we have to be constantly attentive, with a totally open mind. It is only with such an attitude that we will receive everything the teachings have to offer. The problem is that we all have preconceived ideas. As soon as we hear something that fits our own ideas, we think, "Now there's an interesting idea! That's very pleasant." When we hear something that goes contrary to our ideas, opinions, and beliefs, either we distort what we hear until it harmonizes with what we think and can nod, "There, that's the way it should be understood!" or we reject it altogether, branding it as completely incomprehensible. This is not the correct approach for a student who sincerely wishes to learn. A serious student must open his or her mind completely and try to understand the teachings as they are, without distorting them.

This is not to say that we should not use our intelligence—we should. But first we should listen and try to understand what is being said.

We should note that a fruitful practice is the best gift we can give our spiritual friend because the more we practice, the better we practice, the more we attest to his teaching abilities. The Tibetan tradition attaches great importance to what is called the transmission lineage, through which a particular teaching is passed on from master to disciple from one generation to the next. What we call the lineage holder is the person who trains the best students. A realized and very accomplished master is not necessarily the holder of the lineage;[9] it is the best teacher who will be the lineage holder.

Often we are asked if it is possible to know which teacher will suit a particular student and if the teacher knows it. All depends on the quality and degree of realization of the teacher. The best are those capable of understanding what is happening in the mind of the student, but they are very rare. Some people have such a strong karmic relationship with a teacher that just to hear his name is enough to fill them with devotion. Such was Milarepa's case when he heard the name of Marpa, and Gampopa's when he heard the name of Milarepa. If we feel devotion, faith, and strong sympathy for someone, perhaps we have a certain karmic link with him or her and we could ask the teacher to become our lama. However, in a general way, according to Buddhist scriptures, the first thing to do is verify whether the teacher is genuine by referring to the qualities mentioned earlier.

Finding a perfect master is without doubt rare and difficult, but if we find a teacher endowed with most of these qualities, we can certainly ask him or her to become our guide. If he has but a few of these qualities, perhaps it is wiser to refrain. Anyway, it is important to remember that no matter how great the knowledge and qualities of the chosen teacher, in the end it is the student who must learn and practice. One's own studies and practice are the most important factors.

RECEIVING THE TEACHINGS IN THE RIGHT WAY

Gampopa compares the right attitude of a sincere student to that of a sick person anxious to get well as quickly as possible. The spiritual friend, the teacher, is the doctor and the teaching is the treatment. Understanding and practicing the Dharma is like following a course of treatment and taking one's medication.

In the Vajrayana, it is often said that disciples must have total, unlimited confidence in their master. Some people find this statement disturbing. It must be understood correctly. It is true that the purer vision of our guru we have, the better student we become. It is said that if we see our master as a buddha, we will become a buddha. If we consider him to be someone very talented, a great scholar or a great saint, we will also become a great scholar or a great saint; whereas if we see him as no different from ourselves, we will remain as we are. It is for this reason that great importance is given to choosing one's teacher. If our examination, our critical judgment, is faulty, we are lost. Finding the right spiritual friend is the most important thing in a life. When we have found him, we have already made half the journey.

If it is so important to choose one's master well, it is also important not to waste too much time before making a decision, as this story illustrates. Long ago, a Chinese emperor invited Sakya Pandita, a great Tibetan lama, to his court. When Sakya Pandita arrived, the emperor announced that he had to examine whether he was worthy of becoming his master. He examined him for three years and finally declared that he accepted him as his master. Sakya Pandita replied that he, in turn, had to decide whether he could accept the emperor as a disciple. He died before giving his answer.

You should accept someone as your guru only when you are completely sure that he or she is the right guru for you. If you choose the right person, your spiritual teacher will not ask you to do anything reprehensible like killing or stealing. If you are given an instruction that you don't understand or that you feel is not correct, the scriptures say clearly that you can refuse and tell your master that you are unable to do what he is asking. It is not compulsory to blindly obey everything that your master tells you to do. You can then tell him that you are not prepared to do as he asks. If your master cannot accept it, he is indubitably not the master who suits you.

In following the path of the bodhisattvas, we should go at our own pace, according to our own level. Accomplished bodhisattvas should certainly be capable of giving all they have, even their lives, for the benefit of others. However, this does not mean that having taken the bodhisattva vows, we should at once be able to sacrifice our life for others! That's not the point. The scriptures say that if we don't mind giving away a bowl of curry, we should give it. When what we feel for our body is no different from what we feel for a bowl of curry, we can also give away our body if necessary! This is how we proceed: progressively.

4. THE METHOD:

The Instructions of the Spiritual Friend

If we are fortunate enough to have the first three conditions, why haven't we become buddhas yet? Gampopa mentions four obstacles that prevent us from realizing enlightenment.

The first three obstacles are excessive attachment to this life, to the pleasures of samsara, and to the peace of nirvana. The fourth is ignorance of the path that leads to buddhahood. Nonetheless, an experienced spiritual friend's instructions should help us to overcome all four of them.

There is a specific antidote for each obstacle. Meditating on impermanence allows us to shed the feeling of being overly attached to the experiences of this life. Contemplating and understanding the nature of samsara and its inherent sufferings, karma and its results, helps us to reduce our attachment to the sensual pleasures of this world. By developing loving-kindness and compassion, we can overcome the egotistical wish to find the peace of meditation and nirvana and to get out of samsara alone. If we see the logic of compassion we will naturally try to attain enlightenment in order to help other beings. Lastly, developing *bodhichitta* dissipates our ignorance of how to become buddhas.

In a way, all the instructions of the Buddha and the teachers who followed him are included in these four topics. Of these four recommendations, the fourth is the most important. According to Mahayana Buddhism, bodhichitta includes all the methods and techniques of the Buddhist path. Every teaching of the Buddha is related either to the cause of bodhichitta, or to the way to attain it, or to its results, or else to bodhichitta itself. There is no Buddhist teaching that is not linked to bodhichitta in one way or another.

FIRST ANTIDOTE

Contemplating Impermanence

Buddha said that everything compounded is impermanent. Everything that isn't made of one single substance but of different elements must, by its very nature, fall apart. It is a natural law: there is no substance that is not composite. As a result, everything in this world is impermanent. We can conclude that whoever is born will die, whatever is accumulated will be exhausted, whatever is built up will fall to ruin, and whoever come together will part sooner or later. Nothing compounded remains unchanged. That is why we must understand that everything is impermanent. Contemplating impermanence is, in fact, considered the best meditation. Buddha said: "Of all footprints, those of the elephant are the broadest and the deepest. Similarly, of all meditations, that on impermanence is the strongest and the most beneficial."

If we understand impermanence at its deepest level, we also understand the philosophy of emptiness (shunyata), because they are the same thing. If we understand interdependence, we also understand karma, the law of action and reaction. If we have a deep understanding of impermanence and interdependence, we also understand the notion of rebirth, of successive lives.

Another result of this understanding of impermanence is that it will make us less attached to our present life, less unhappy, easier to live with, and more carefree and relaxed. In fact, most of the problems we encounter in this world come from the idea of permanence. Why do we fight with each other? Why are there so many conflicts between religions, countries, races, and so on? Because we believe that situations last, because we see them as permanent. It seems to us that everything can stay the way it is for a very long time and that therefore we have to fight to change situations by force and win people over to our cause. If we truly understood impermanence, we would not act that way. During an interfaith conference for peace in Delhi, a speaker commented that if world leaders, politicians, and religious heads all put a greater emphasis on impermanence, there would be no more conflicts and wars. I think he was right.

There are different methods for meditating on impermanence.

The first is to contemplate the impermanence of the outside world going from general to specific, from infinitely large to infinitely small. Let's think about the world, the way it has changed since its beginning, its formation, its evolution, and how it will eventually disintegrate: this earth, the sun, the moon, everything will one day be completely destroyed. Even the galaxies, the planets, the stars come into being, evolve, and die.

There are not only large changes but also a multitude of small changes like the succession of seasons, of days and nights, of sunshine and rain. Time never stops. Each moment brings something new. Nothing stays motionless in space; everything changes all the time. Contemplating and understanding this motion is meditating on the impermanence of the outside world.

Now, let's look at the beings who inhabit the earth: we see them be born, grow old, and die, which should remind us of our own impermanence. Death is how impermanence reveals itself the most strikingly

to us. The contemplation of death helps us fully realize what impermanence means. Everyone, absolutely everyone must die. Even if there is
no certainty as to the time of our death, there is absolutely no doubt
that we will have to die and that nothing at all will be able to stop this
process. It is important to remind ourselves that we can die at any moment. Nagarjuna once said, "If I breathe out and do not breathe in
again, I am dead! Isn't it marvelous to think that even while I am sleeping at night, I do not stop breathing and in the morning, I am still
alive?" And it is true. Life is so precarious that if we breathe out and do
not breathe back in again, we are dead!

We can also apprehend how fragile our existence is by reminding
ourselves that our body is composed of many parts and substances and
is therefore very unstable. Our life is decreasing every moment, and
nothing increases it! Like an arrow shot by an archer, it continues on its
way toward the target, without ever stopping. In the same way, every
passing second brings us inexorably closer to death. The causes of
death are numerous, whereas there are few to support life. Even the factors that generally sustain our life, like medicine and food, can also
sometimes cause our death. Life is fragile because we can die at any
moment. Youth, health, a desirable social position, wealth, numerous
friends, and fame are no guarantee or protection against death. We
must understand and accept that when death comes, nothing, no outer
or inner force, can stop it. We should take this fact into consideration,
and from now on, our actions should not only aim at the well-being of
our body in this life but also have a much longer-term goal. There is no
doubt that our life will come to an end and that we will die. Trying to
ignore this would be madness. It is better to face reality than to hide behind the illusion that no change will affect us or that everything will
sort itself out.

Too often, people consider that thinking about death is sinister and
depressing, that it is better not to talk or even think about it. Some people go as far as to believe that simply talking about it brings bad luck.
The deaths of others frighten us and make us feel insecure because they
remind us of what we all know, even if we wish to forget it. Nonethe-

less, examining the subject more thoroughly will not make us more unhappy or depressed. On the contrary, we will be more at peace because if we really face this reality, we will understand it more deeply and behave accordingly in our daily lives.

Let me tell you a little story about this. During the life of the Buddha, a very close-knit family suddenly lost a son who was already married. The neighbors came to express their condolences, thinking they would find the family mourning. They were surprised and shocked to discover that, far from being plunged into great suffering, they all seemed perfectly serene. The parents were going about their usual activities; the wife was coming back singing from the river where she had fetched water. The neighbors asked them why they were not grieving, and each replied in his or her own way, "Knowing that everything is impermanent and that we are together in this family for a short time, we try to respect and love each other. We know that we will be separated sooner or later, and for the time given us to live together, we try to be good to each other and live in harmony. We never hurt him or did him any wrong during his life, nor did he us, so we have no regrets. We know that he is going his own way, according to his own karma. This is why we are still very happy and our mourning is peaceful."

This simple story shows very well that the understanding of impermanence and death shouldn't make anyone unhappy—quite the contrary. Many people who have gone through near-death experiences say that they now appreciate life much more because they have understood impermanence. If we are not confronted with death, we don't value our life. Our small daily problems seem so important that we usually forget how precious life itself is, whereas when we confront death, those small problems become terribly insignificant! If we truly, deeply understand that everything is impermanent and transitory, our attachment to this life will diminish and our faith in the Dharma will grow. We will be motivated to diligently practice the path leading out of the sufferings of samsara. Understanding impermanence will also help us to get less involved in attachment and aversion. We will have a broader general approach, be more open-minded, and become wiser in a way. We will not make mountains out of molehills anymore. We will stop getting involved in petty arguments, which are a sign of a narrow and irritable mind. And we will not let ourselves be affected and disturbed by small things. We will take highs and lows, happiness and unhappiness less seriously. In a nutshell, this clearer and more detached view of the world, of samsara, will reduce our psychological problems.

Some people ask if those who have had near-death experiences entered what we call in Tibetan Buddhism the "*bardo* of death."[1] It is not easy to assert anything about this because the situation differs from one case to another. It is usually said that a person can go all the way to what we call physical death—that is, the dissolution of the elements (earth, water, fire, air)—and still come back. Next comes the inner death, which corresponds to the dissolution of thoughts, of all the mental factors. Once this process is completed, it is said that the person cannot come back anymore.

However, certain stories of transference of consciousness from one body to another make these things more difficult to assess. Here is one of these stories.

Do Khyentse was a holy man in Tibet, a yogi who had reached a very high level of spiritual realization. However, his very unconventional behavior made many people wonder about him, and some skeptical monks thought he was simply crazy. Two of them decided to test him. They waited for him to come along. One pretended to be dead and the other rushed toward the yogi, pleading with tears in his eyes that he practice *phowa* (transference of consciousness) for his unfortunate friend who had just drowned. The yogi nodded his agreement and, without any ritual or prayer, simply snapped his fingers and went away. Laughing, the monk called to his friend from afar that he could get up, for Do Khyentse was really only a charlatan without any power or knowledge. But his friend didn't get up. Shaking him was no good. He was really dead. Terrified, the monk ran after the yogi and threw himself at his feet, confessing his error, his stupidity, and his blindness, begging him to bring his friend's consciousness back into his body. The yogi then emptied the pipe he had been smoking on the dead monk's forehead. The monk soon got up and bitterly blamed his friend for bringing him back to this lowly world, when he was going to a magnificent place! So it is perhaps possible, despite everything, to leave one's body and then come back to it. . . .

SECOND ANTIDOTE

Contemplating the Misery of Samsara

As long as we are in the samsaric state of mind, we will not find complete satisfaction and happiness. Samsara is suffering by definition. It is a state of mind characterized by the presence of varying degrees of the three types of suffering. Therefore, we need to get out of it. Fortunately, this is possible. That is the point of contemplating the misery of samsara.

The Three Types of Suffering

The first form of suffering is what Guenther translated as the "suffering of conditioned existence." A literal translation of the Tibetan would be the "suffering inherent to all that is composite."[2] Most people do not even notice this suffering. Everything changes all the time, but we are conditioned to believe the opposite. We cling to this belief, thinking that it brings happiness and security, but even the things we most cling to, the ones that seem to bring us the most stability, are transient. We are not free but conditioned and stuck in our own karma. We are constantly controlled, without knowing it, by innumerable causes and results, which we ourselves have created. Without any control or even awareness of this phenomenon, we cannot escape from it. This lack of freedom keeps us from enjoying total happiness.

The second type of suffering is called the suffering of change.[3] This is the anxiety that accompanies our anticipation of change. When we are in an ideal situation in an idyllic place, we are already dreading change. Even while enjoying a moment of happiness, our mind already fears losing it, which is in itself suffering.

The third type of suffering is called the suffering of suffering.[4] This is "real" suffering, the kind we experience when we are sick, when we are about to die, when we lose what we love, or when we are confronted with what we hate. It is what we usually call suffering.

These three types of suffering are constantly with us. We are never free from them. Their presence is the very definition of samsara.

The first type of suffering is a neutral experience in terms of sensation. We are unconscious of this process because it does not cause either pain or pleasure. The second type of suffering is linked to the fear that comes with feelings of comfort, of well-being. The third type of suffering is a real experience of pain. Yet if we look deeply at them, all three are experiences of suffering. For the last two types of suffering, this is easy to understand. On the other hand, the suffering inherent to conditioned existence is very subtle. If it is a neutral experience, how can we define it as suffering? I will use a comparison. Suppose we are suffering from a serious illness and at the same time from a small cut on the hand or foot. As long as the main pain is sharp, as long as we are in the grip of a strong fever, we will not feel the minor pains. But as soon as the fever comes down, we begin to feel the cuts. In the same way, the second and third types of suffering keep us from perceiving the subtle conditions of our karma, which truly chain us. Only when we are freed from our grossest sufferings do we become conscious of the subtle conditions of our enslavement.

A passage from *The Commentary on the Abhidharma* says: "Just one hair, gone from the palm of the hand into the eye, generates discomfort and suffering; the immature, like the palm of the hand, do not understand the suffering inherent to conditioned existence, whereas realized beings, who are like the eye, do see the suffering inherent to the composite." The first type of suffering is omnipresent, and even if we do not notice its presence, it is the chain that hampers us the most.

The constant change we experience in our lives is part of the same process, like the string of rebirths. Each change is conditioned by a multitude of factors. All phenomena are conditioned by each other. We are continually carried, pushed forward with little personal choice. Of course, we have a certain degree of choice, but this choice itself is conditioned as long as our mind is not free from attachment and the other mind poisons. The pressures and demands of modern life can give us an idea of the limits of our room for maneuvering.

Gampopa illustrates his point with numerous examples, but I don't think it's necessary to look at all of them. Actually, it's enough to open our eyes to see the suffering all around us.

Rebirth

Gampopa also warns us of the danger of being attached to our problems and the risk of drowning in our own sufferings. We must understand their true nature. After defining what suffering is, Gampopa describes the specific way it manifests in each of the six realms. He warns us against the attachment we might feel for one or another of these realms and, on the other hand, encourages us to develop the firm determination to break with suffering, leave samsaric existence far behind us, and reach true enlightenment.

Here we come to the question of rebirth. It is sometimes difficult for Westerners to integrate this idea, as rebirth is not part of their cultural background. It is actually only one aspect of interdependence and the lack of intrinsic existence of self and phenomena. For someone who comes from a culture where this idea goes without saying, it seems just as strange not to believe in it! Actually, almost all the life forms around us go through this process of rebirth. Let's take flowers, grass, and trees, for example: everything around us dies and is reborn again and again. This flower is the result of the previous one. One flower wilts, its roots dig down into the earth, and when the right conditions come together—earth, water, sun—another flower is born from the same root. Almost all the life forms around us repeat this cycle.

According to Buddhism, our successive lives are not like a necklace where each life is a bead and the string is the soul going through all of them. The Buddhist philosophy denies the existence of a spirit or a soul that goes from one body to the next, as if one changes clothes (even if sometimes this is what is presented in the beginning to help people understand the process). When we go on to the next life, nothing is transferred, nothing goes from one place to another. To illustrate this essential point, Gampopa gives eight examples, but we will look at only four of them.

The first example is of yogurt. How does milk become yogurt? Milk is not yogurt and yogurt is not milk. When it is milk there is not yet yogurt and when it becomes yogurt there is no longer milk. There can't be yogurt without milk, but milk disappears when yogurt appears. It is not that something goes out of milk and enters yogurt. So, nothing really goes out of us. Our present conditions create our next moment as well as our next life.

Another example is the mirror. When we look in a mirror, we see a reflection in it, but how does that image appear there? Our face does not travel—no part of our face is transferred into the mirror—yet its form appears, and without our own face, there would be no reflection in the mirror.

Now let's suppose a candle is lit and we light a second candle with the first. How does the flame go from one to the other? If we watch a candle flame, it burns constantly, from the beginning until the candle is completely burned down. Is it the same flame or not? Is there one flame, or are there many?

Let's take another example. At this moment I'm here. Why? Because I was here the moment before. Why am I here? I could say it is because I was born. Actually, if I had never been born, I wouldn't be here at all. My birth is one of the numerous factors of my presence here. If I was born but didn't grow up, if I had died young, I wouldn't be here either. My youth is therefore the cause of my presence here. I can also answer that if I'm here, it's because of yesterday. I didn't die yesterday, and so

I'm still here. My presence here and now is the result of my past. However, that past doesn't mean that I've always been the way I am. Therefore, one can't talk about a "self."

From the Buddhist point of view of rebirth, in the same way that the present moment produces the next, this present life is the cause of the next one. The last moment produces the next moment. This is not different from the way a flower grows. What we are now was created, conditioned by our past. If we hadn't been children, we wouldn't be the adults we are now. Yet we are no longer that child: we may have some white hair, some wrinkles. That child and we are "one" and at the same time different. Our present life and our future life have a similar relationship. The present circumstances, our situation, our actions, our present thoughts produce the next moment. The circumstances, actions, and thoughts of the next moment condition the following moment and so on. So what we are now conditions our future. It is a continuous process, and it proves that since I'm here now, I was here yesterday and the day before. How can we know that we were alive yesterday? How do we know it with certainty? What's the proof? Yesterday could have been just a dream! Our only proof of having existed yesterday is that we exist today. If we were not here today, we couldn't have been anywhere yesterday. The proof of tomorrow is our existence today. We don't disappear. We'll also be here tomorrow, but perhaps in another form.

Our body changes. Everything changes. Our feeling of "I am," "what I was when I was a child," "that child was me," "I will be that old person" is our self-identification. It's the main element that links us to our identity and continues in the next life. Whether we see ourselves as a child, an adult, or an old person, we think, "This is me." In the same way, in our next life, we will think, "This is me," even if the conditions have changed.

Our emotions, our actions, our karma constantly create numerous conditions. These conditions won't suddenly disappear at our death. When one shoots an arrow, it continues its trajectory and necessarily falls somewhere. It will not suddenly vaporize in midair! These conditions must be contained in a future, in a later event. There must therefore be a continuation, which is the next life. This is how we explain the series of existences. The next life will not, however, be exactly the same. We will be different from who we are in this life. Nothing of our body nor of our mind is transferred from one life to another. The next life is caused, created by our present conditioning. It is not an exact reproduction of what we are now.

This is also what explains how, according to Buddhist philosophy, if we understand the nonexistence of ego, we could manifest in two, three, four, or one hundred different incarnations. So it is said that a being who has reached the first *bhumi*[5] can manifest as one hundred emanations. Whoever has reached the second bhumi can manifest as one hundred thousand and so on in growing numbers. What that means is that our freedom grows proportionately to our understanding of the true nature of things and that we acquire control over mind and matter.

The process of death is a dissolution. Life, the body, the mind—everything dissolves. The next mental structure is the product of this process and so on, at each moment. In the same way, our previous life was not identical to the life we lead now, but it was not completely different either. What we are is the product of our previous life. Someone who was very interested in spirituality in the last life probably has the same propensity in this life. This is what we call karmic imprints.[6] Different karmic imprints create different categories of people.

This may lead some to fall into the trap of a passive attitude, thinking, "I am the result of my past, and since what I am is the consequence of karmic imprints, I can't do anything about it." Of course, we can't change what we are now, because we already are what we are. There is nothing we can do about it because it is the result of our past. But we can partially control what we will be in the future. If the past made our present, our present can in turn make our future. What we can be in the next moment, next year, or next life is in our hands, right now!

The Six Realms

Contrary to what some Westerners tend to think, there is no particular destiny attached to specific actions. Let's take suicide as an example. Committing suicide means taking a life, which is considered to be very negative. However, from a Buddhist point of view, what we do or do not do is not the only criterion determining whether an action is considered good, bad, or very bad. The essential criterion is the underlying motivation for the action.

We need to correctly understand the theory of karma. Karma is the conditioning that we create: whatever we do, any action will have consequences. Karma develops from this conditioning, which directly creates the next moment. Karma is not the long-term result of what we do now: it is a process of actions and reactions. The effects can be felt in the short or long term, but the most important thing is to understand that whatever we do, there will be consequences.

The same goes for the six realms. For example, rebirth in a hell realm is the result of our conditioning. Hatred, anger, and our negative thoughts become more real, more tangible, and we thus find ourselves in a hell world. It isn't a place where one is sent. In a single place, different beings can experience the hells, paradise, or the human world. Take, for instance, water: it is perceived in a very different way by the beings who inhabit each of the six realms. A human will see it as a refreshing drink, a hell being as molten metal, and a hungry ghost as poison; a fish will consider it as its living environment, and a god will see it as a nectar of long life and beauty. These different viewpoints are simply the result of our own conditioning, our own chain of karmic actions and reactions. According to Buddhism, these different realms are states of mind generated by the six negative emotions. Beings dominated by hatred and anger will be reborn in the hells. Very greedy beings will be born in the realm of hungry ghosts. The predominance of desire is the cause of rebirth in the human world. If ignorance, stupidity, and confusion are dominant, one is born as an animal. If jealousy is very strong, one is born in the world of the jealous demigods. If pride is predominant, one is then born among the gods. These six negative emotions characterize the six states of mind that constitute what we call samsara.

We need to perceive and recognize the three types of suffering that pervade the six realms, wherever we are born and whatever our life form. Within samsara, there is neither complete happiness nor total freedom. The only way to reach them is to liberate ourselves from the samsaric state of mind by realizing the true quality of buddha nature and by developing it. This realization frees us completely from confusion and false beliefs and leads us to enlightenment.

Understanding Karma

The three forms of suffering mentioned in the preceding chapter are the fruit of karma. *The Hundred Karmas Sutra*[7] explains how the different types of karma create the great variety of living beings. According to Buddhism, everything is created by karma; nothing is the creation of an all-powerful being. Everything we do produces its own effect, its own result. No super-being or god is pleased or displeased with what we do and rewards or punishes our positive or negative actions. The law of karma, which is actually the law of interdependence, can be stated this way: Everything we do will have consequences. A positive action will have positive results. A negative action will have negative results. Nothing and no one decides to reward or punish us. It is the force of the action itself that brings about the corresponding result.

The interaction of all the actions we take is complex, as the following story illustrates. An old woman had just listened to the teachings about the results of karma at the nearby monastery. Talking about the benefits of positive action, the lama had claimed that even a small positive action would have great results and that, for example, thanks to a single recitation of the name of Buddha Amitabha, one would be reborn in the pure land of Sukhavati.[8] Speaking about the negative effects of bad actions, he had said that the smallest error, even a simple lie, was enough to plunge one into the hells for thousands of cosmic eons. The old woman, perplexed, went to the lama and asked him, "If what you said about the results of good deeds is true, not only lamas but even I won't fail to become buddha in this life. On the other hand, if I believe what you said about bad actions, not only I but even you will surely go to hell! So, where do we stand?"

In fact, none of us behaves completely positively or negatively. Our behavior, our karmas are composed of so many mismatched elements all bound up together, the negative with the positive, that the results are also extremely complex. It is said that each of the colors of a peacock's feather has its own karmic cause. Only a fully realized being is able to determine precisely which is the cause of what. No one acts in a totally positive or negative way, and therefore the fruits we harvest are mixed.

The notion of karma is often misunderstood and confused with fatalism, the passive acceptance of our destiny. Karma is then seen as a force pulling us along like a bale of straw on the ocean of life. However, this is not the Buddhist theory of karma, which is not completely deterministic but much more dynamic.

The law of karma is nothing other than the law of interdependence, of conditioned arising. As was explained in the previous section, what we are now is the result of our past, of the karma that we have accumulated. The force of this karma shaped us and set the limits of what we are now. That explains why we are not always able to accomplish what we would like to. Of course, we are limited, but, within the form, the space that is ours, we have the choice to act in a certain way or not. Our future is in our hands now. What we do now will create our future. This is the law of karma. Each person has his or her own karma, or to be more exact, *is* his or her own karma.

In addition to personal karma, there's also what is called collective karma. The world we live in is the product of the collective karma of its inhabitants. The beings who share the same levels of karmic existence are able to communicate with each other, which they couldn't do if they lived in different worlds. However, the way beings act within a certain karmic level and the way they are affected individually by global events depend on their personal karma.

How Do We Accumulate Karma?

We accumulate karma by the law of cause and effect, or action-reaction. According to the *Abhidharmakosha*, there are two types of action, two facets of accumulation of karma, which in Tibetan we call *sempele*[9] and *sampele*.[10]

The first factor is the activity of mind, thought, intention. *Sempe-le* means thinking without acting. Actually, each action begins in our mind. Without an initial thought, no action is possible. This is the karma of the mind, of motivation. We do not put it into action, but the motivation is already there. The second factor, *sampe-le,* means putting the thought into action, either physically or verbally.

These different categories of deeds can have three sorts of effects: positive, negative, or neutral karma. Negative karma is the result of a truly harmful act, such as killing, lying, or stealing. We speak of the ten harmful actions, which are among the main causes of negative karma. Positive karma is the product of good actions, like giving, protecting life, leading a virtuous life and so forth. Neutral karma springs from our inaction, as when we sleep or when we are in *samadhi*.[11] We don't create any karma then, either negative or positive.

The Three Types of Karmic Results

We distinguish three types of results.

The first is called the direct result, or the result of maturation. Take, for example, the murder, committed with hatred, of an exceptional person who has been very kind to us. The direct result of such a horrible action could be, for example, to be reborn in the hells or to undergo very great suffering.

The second type of result is what we call the similar condition. Just as the direct result of such a murder would be rebirth in hell, the similar condition would be rebirth in the human world but with a short life. Because of the similarity of condition, one would die violently, of an accident, an attack, or a similar event.

The third type of result includes the secondary effects. To take our example, after the direct consequence of rebirth in hell and having experienced similar conditions, one could still undergo secondary effects, such as being born in a very turbulent, unstable place where famine and war are raging.

The Four Ways Karma Matures

Although this is not mentioned in Gampopa's text, it is useful to specify the four ways that karma matures.

The first is immediate. The action is immediately followed by its result. We hit someone and he hits us back. We insult someone and he replies straight away. This boomerang effect happening during one life is called the immediate result.

The second way is when the result is not immediately visible in this life but occurs in the next life.

The third way is when the result is produced in an unspecified future, as the act committed was not very strong.

The fourth way is when it is not clear whether the action will have a result or not. It is so weak that it may not have any significant consequence.

The four ways that karma ripens depend on the strength and the motivation behind the action. The stronger the emotion, the motivation, the aspiration are, the more noticeable the result.

The importance of the strength of our motivation shows that our future is not totally determined by our past actions. Suppose that, due to the karma associated with our past actions, we are supposed to act in a certain way. If our present motivation goes in the opposite direction and is very strong, the consequence of our negative karma can be postponed or even avoided and we can then take a new direction. When the stronger motivation overpowers the weaker, it is an example of what we call the immediate result. Naturally, these mechanisms also apply to positive actions.

Breaking the Chain of Karma

As long as we are prisoners of this process of karmic accumulation, whether the karma is negative or positive, we are chained to samsara. Creating positive, then negative, then neutral karma, we go around in circles, up and down, in the confusion of samsara. However, all karmas are temporary: the results appear and disappear. They are not part of us; they are adventitious and temporary. It is therefore possible for us to completely break the chain and free ourselves.

All karma, whether positive or negative, can be purified. Even the most negative karma can be washed off when we sincerely regret what we have done and commit ourselves to not doing it again. We then replace negative karma with positive karma.

But we can go even further, and the best thing we can do is to break the chain of karma once and for all. This is possible if we completely eliminate our ignorance, which is the illusion of ego. Conquering our ignorance, our confusion, liberates us from the grip of ego. As soon as there is no longer "anyone" to experience the results of karma, its chain is broken. Without accumulation of karma, there are no more karmic results.

Here is a story to illustrate this point. During the Buddha's lifetime, the king Ajatashatru killed his father, who was a holy arhat. Later, under the influence of Devadatta, a jealous cousin of the Buddha, he attempted to kill the Buddha himself. Luckily, he wasn't able to commit this heinous act. The years went by and he came to understand the horror of his crimes. Full of remorse, he repented and begged the Buddha to send him someone to hear his confession and help him to purify himself. The Buddha sent him Manjushri, who, instead of reassuring him, promised him the blackest hell, without the least hope of release. Ajatashatru was desperate. When he reached the very deepest despair,

Manjushri asked him suddenly: "Look closely. Who is going to burn in hell? What, in you, will really be going to hell? What, or who?"

Ajashatru looked and eventually, in an instant, realized his true nature. He saw that he was not an independent unit that would go to hell, but an aggregate and an arising from many causes and conditions; almost a process. In an instant, he had realized the true nature of himself. All at once he had broken the karmic chain and liberated himself completely. He had reached the first level of realization.

The main aim of Dharma is to break the karmic chain, to break this attachment, this grasping, this identification, which is the very root of samsara. Reducing the identification with a self, the attachment to this idea of ego, allows us to let go, to relax. We can at last put down a useless burden we have been carrying for too long.

This is very important to understand, even as far as our daily life is concerned, and particularly in the West, where the psychological approach tends to explain every problem in relation to childhood experiences. According to the Buddhist approach, it's the memory, the attachment to memories that is the real source of problems. In fact, you're no longer that child who was mistreated, unloved, misunderstood. That suffering only affects you now because you think you still are that person. If you didn't grasp at those memories, if you didn't identify with the child that you once were, those past experiences would no longer matter and couldn't affect you. They would simply be memories of events that happened to someone else. As soon as we understand that the past is past, that it's simply a memory, we instantly relieve ourselves of problems that we have been carrying around with us for too long.

Therefore, let's try to understand and deeply realize shunyata. Understanding and experiencing absolute truth is the ultimate weapon that can cut off the chain of karma.

However, it is also very important to know that, at the same time, we must under no circumstances ignore karma or minimize its effects. As long as we experience an ego, we are in confusion and ignorance, and therefore under the power of the effects of karma. Consequently, let's be as careful as possible to accumulate good karma and avoid negative karma, while trying to develop our understanding of ultimate reality. These instructions are the pith instructions of the Kadampa lamas.

THIRD ANTIDOTE

Love and Compassion

If our goal in life is just limited to our own peace, our own liberation, we will never achieve the full realization of our buddha nature. According to Mahayana Buddhism, limiting oneself to one's own liberation from the sufferings of samsara is a trap. It is not the best path. We need to develop love and compassion, because it is our true nature and the only way to fully develop and awaken ourselves.

What we call love here is different from the notion of romantic love. It is the aspiration, the intention expressed by the wish "May all sentient beings be happy." For a bodhisattva, loving is wishing happiness for all, for oneself as well as for others. The starting point for developing love is realizing that if it is right for oneself to feel happy, then it is equally right for all other sentient beings. When we wish that all beings be freed from suffering, we then speak of compassion. Even though the two concepts are very close and of the same nature, slight nuances justify the distinction.

Love and compassion are among the most important principles of Mahayana Buddhism. A buddha, a realized being, is someone who has developed love/compassion and wisdom to their highest level. Compassion is one of the most important elements for achieving buddhahood. Without compassion, it's impossible to become enlightened.

Not only are love and compassion indispensable for becoming enlightened, but they are also an integral part of buddha nature. In contrast to hatred and other negative emotions, which are temporary and can therefore be purified, compassion is inherent to the ultimate nature of beings. When exploring the deeper forms of compassion, we discover that it is in reality one of the ingredients of the true nature of the buddha mind. The more we develop love and compassion, the more we get rid of negative emotions.

THE DEVELOPMENT OF LOVING-KINDNESS[12]

Gampopa distinguishes three forms of loving-kindness:

1. Toward sentient beings,
2. With reference to the nature of reality, and
3. Without reference to any given object.

Benevolence with reference to sentient beings is what we usually call loving-kindness. We can wonder whether it's possible to generate loving-kindness or not. His Holiness the Dalai Lama answers that it's always possible to develop loving-kindness because, even if we may sometimes feel hate or anger, we also feel love, and it is much nicer and natural to feel love than to feel anger. We feel angry when we are disturbed. We feel love when we are not disturbed because love comes to us more naturally. We don't feel angry all the time and, as love and hate are mutually exclusive, we should try to prolong the moments when we feel love. If we succeed, we will eventually feel nothing but love. As loving-kindness and anger cannot coexist, it's sufficient to develop one in order for the other to disappear. It's like hot and cold: one can't feel hot and cold at the same time. Negative emotions come and go. If we don't allow negative emotions to manifest, they will not develop. At the same time, if we habituate ourselves to feeling loving-kindness, we'll feel it more and more often.

If Buddhism defines love as the wish that all sentient beings be happy, the starting point for developing this loving-kindness is to realize that, if we wish happiness for ourselves, all other beings have exactly the same desire. However, I'm aware that, in the West, a certain number of people claim not to love themselves. How then can they develop love for others? Nevertheless, I think that most probably these people expect too much of themselves and feel very guilty not to be up to the high standards they set for themselves. This guilt, the blame they put on themselves, prevents them from becoming conscious of the love they actually feel for themselves.

How to Deal with Hatred

To pacify hate is the first stage in developing love. To succeed, we must first of all understand that feeling hate is absurd. We hate people because they harmed us, whether they meant to or not, and we feel hurt. However, they hurt us because they actually have no free choice. In some cases, they really believe they're doing the right thing. They allow events and circumstances to control them, or they find themselves swayed by strong and uncontrollable emotions. They've lost control of themselves. Someone completely submerged by emotions is like a madman or a drunk, who can't be considered completely responsible for his or her actions. We don't take a drunk's or a mad person's words or acts seriously. We should treat people who harm us the same way.

Perhaps we are wounded by unpleasant words or actions, but the one who will suffer most from their effects is the person who actually harmed us. Indeed, this person is the one who, under the influence of negative emotions, accumulates negative karma that will have negative consequences. If we believe in the law of karma, we understand that someone who harms others will suffer the painful consequences, not through any outer intervention, but through the force of the act itself. Such a person is therefore more to be pitied than hated, and we have no reason not to forgive him or her. On the other hand, we have a good reason to feel compassion for him or her. Seen from this angle, hatred becomes almost illogical. That does not mean that we shouldn't try to stop the person from harming us or himself, but we do not need to hate him.

Hatred means defeat, whereas loving-kindness is a victory. Swami Vivekananda, an Indian sage, was traveling by train in India. A very bad-tempered passenger did all he could to insult him. Swami Vivekananda didn't respond. When the passenger got tired of insulting him, the swami asked him, "If someone offers you a gift but you refuse it, who gets the gift?" The passenger replied, "The person who gave it." The Swami then said, "I don't accept anything you said." Not answering hate with hate is a victory because hate generates tension and unpleasant sensations, while love brings peace. Free from hatred, from jealousy, greed, and discontent, we can be happy, peaceful, and comfortable in the warmth of kindness. Love is peaceful and generates a positive attitude. When nothing negative bothers us, we feel light, free, and relaxed. Those around us will also feel this warmth and be aware of our benevolence. Warm people, those with a kind heart, make everybody wish to speak to them, to be close to them.

Extending Loving-Kindness to All Beings

To generate loving-kindness and a generous heart not only means getting rid of hatred but also wishing that all beings achieve happiness.

The traditional Tibetan method to achieve this is based on the feeling of gratitude. To me it seems only natural to want to reciprocate goodness to those who are generous toward us. Starting from this feeling, we learn to gradually extend this benevolence to all beings. The logic underlying this approach is that it's possible to gradually extend to others the intense love we feel for one person, so as to finally include all other sentient beings.

I don't know if this approach makes sense to you because, in reading Western books or watching Western films, I don't get the impression that gratitude or the desire to return the kindnesses shown to us plays a great role in Western society, while it's a major preoccupation with Tibetans and, I think, in Oriental society in general. In a culture such as mine, this attitude is deeply anchored. For example, when people die they regret not having had the time or the opportunity to repay kindnesses accorded them, and their last wishes are often that their relatives repay these debts of the heart. Nevertheless, the absence of such preoccupations in films or literature doesn't mean that Western people don't feel gratitude on a personal level.

In the Tibetan and Indian tradition, the mother is the best example of love, because she is the person who helps us in the least selfish manner. She's the one who did, or tried to do, her best, sacrificing her own comfort and best interests for us. This is why we feel love when thinking of our mother.

I think it is interesting to read the passage in which Gampopa describes the role of a mother:

> Remembering kindness is the root of love. Thus one considers the kindness of sentient beings. In this context, the one who has been kindest of all to us in this life is our own mother. In what way? She has been kind by generating our body, kind through undergoing hardships, kind by nurturing our life force, and kind in teaching us the ways of the world. The *Prajnaparamita Sutra in Eight Thousand Verses* says: "Why is this? This mother gave birth to us, she underwent hardships, she gave us our lives and taught us all about the world."

The Kindness of Creating Our Body

This body of ours did not start out fully grown in size, its flesh fully developed and with a healthy complexion. It developed inside our mother through the different embryonic and fetal stages, being gradually created and nourished by vital fluids coming from her very own flesh and blood. It grew thanks to the nourishment coming from the food she ate. It came into being by her having to put up with all sorts of embarrassment, sickness, and suffering. Furthermore, generally speaking, it was she who helped make this body, which started out a tiny infant, into (its present) bulk as big as a yak.

The Kindness of Undergoing Hardships

At first we did not come here clothed, finely adorned, with money in our pocket, and with provision to travel. When we came into this unknown place, where we knew no one at all, we had nothing whatsoever—our only wealth was our howling mouth and our empty stomach. Our mother gave us food so that we would not go hungry, drink to keep us from thirst, clothes to fend off the cold, and wealth to keep us from poverty. It was not as though she just gave us things no longer of use to herself: she herself went without food, without drink, and without new clothes. Furthermore, not only did she sacrifice her happiness as far as this existence is concerned, she also deprived herself of using her assets (as offerings) to provide for her own prosperity in future lives. In brief, without regard to her own happiness in both this life and the next, she devoted herself to rearing and caring for her child.

Nor was it the case that she obtained what was needed easily and pleasurably; to provide for her child she was obliged to sin, to suffer, and to toil. She sinned by having to resort to fishing, killing animals, and so on in order to care for us. She suffered because what she gave her child was the fruit of trading, laboring in the fields, and so forth, wearing (the late evening or early morning) frost for her boots and the stars as a hat, riding the horse of her calves, beaten by the whip of the long grass, her legs exposed to the bites of dogs and her face exposed to the looks of men.

She also treated this stranger who has become her child with more love than her own father, mother, or lama, even though she knew not who this being was or what it would become. She looked at her child with loving eyes, gave her gentle warmth, cradled him in her arms, and talked with sweet words saying, "My joy, ah my sunshine, my treasure, coochi coochi, aren't you mummy's joy," and so forth.

The Kindness of Nurturing Our Life

It is not as though we were born as we are now, knowing how to feed ourselves and endowed with the necessary ability to accomplish difficult tasks. When we were helpless, useless little worms, unable to think, our mother did not discard us but did an inconceivable quantity of things in order to nurture our existence. She took us on her lap, protected us from fire and water, held us away from dangerous precipices, removed all harmful things, and prayed for us. At those times when she feared for our life or health, she resorted to all kinds of doctors, divinations, astrology, exorcisms, recitations of texts, special ceremonies, and so on.

The Kindness of Teaching Us the Ways of the World

At first we were not the clever, experienced, strong-minded people we are now. Apart from being able to bawl and flap our limbs about, we were quite ignorant. When we did not know how to feed ourselves, it was she who taught us how to eat. When we knew not how to dress ourselves, it was she who taught us. When we did not know how to walk, it was she who taught us. When we could not even speak, it was she who taught us, repeating, "Mama, dada," and so on. Having taught us various crafts and skills, she helped us to become a balanced being, strengthening our weaker points and introducing us to the unfamiliar.

What do you think? I am sure that many of you don't agree. Many Westerners are resistant on this matter because of difficulties in their relationship with their mothers. I'd simply like to say that, too often, a mother's love is taken for granted and considered to be something natural. You often expect too much from your parents. You trace the origin of all your problems to your childhood and put the blame on your parents for everything that went wrong.

In a way, this attitude is linked to your lack of belief in reincarnation. Seeing no other possible reason, you think that everything that happens to you can only be the result of events that happened in this present life, during gestation, after your birth, or during your childhood. You think that a mother's love is natural and you accept it as such, without any greater appreciation. You consider all that you receive from your parents as something that they owe you. When your mother gives you everything she has, you think it normal and natural. You don't even acknowledge it. On the other hand, you find it difficult to forgive her smallest selfish act. The slightest error is badly received and you resent her for it. However, if you think of it, a baby is a totally helpless being, at its mother's mercy. She could easily kill it at birth or even before. Infanticide exists. In certain countries, the birth of a daughter is seen as a catastrophe because a dowry must be provided at the moment of marriage; consequently, a baby girl runs a real risk of being killed.

Furthermore, a mother is just a sentient being like everyone else, with her own problems, her own tastes, likes, and dislikes. Suppose a mother abandons her child at birth to follow another man whom she has fallen in love with. We might think that she doesn't love her child, whereas in fact she is only under the influence of a violent passion. We could safely say that she's not really in control of herself. We can of course disapprove of her behavior as a mother, but we have no reason to hate her. Actually, if your mother didn't love or help you, it is her problem. You can't make someone love you. If she loves you and shows you kindness, that's all very well, but she's under no obligation to do so. What have you done to deserve her love? I don't think it is logical to hate someone because he or she doesn't love you! No logical reason justifies all that a mother does for her child. Instead of resenting her for the smallest mistakes she may have committed, we should on the contrary feel grateful to her for all the good things she has given us. I think it's very important to remember this.

Training and Dealing with Emotions

When we encounter difficult and conflicting situations, we're usually too overpowered by our own negative emotions to have the time or the presence of mind to think of love. Simply listening to teachings about love and compassion won't change us immediately or transform us on the spot into perfect bodhisattvas. We will of course flare up in anger again, especially if we're of an angry disposition. We should feel neither guilty nor even uneasy if this happens. What is important is not to get attached to this anger, not to feed it or attempt to justify it. There's a difference between getting angry and feeding anger. Even Tilopa said that the simple fact of being angry doesn't do us much wrong. However, the attachment to anger and the desire for revenge are really bad and can harm us greatly. We should consider what benefit there is in maintaining this anger, in being attached to it. There's none: it only hurts us and hurts others.

By developing loving-kindness, we can gradually change. By remaining vigilant and conscious of the uselessness of anger, we'll be better able to control ourselves. We'll gradually get less and less often angry over little things, and the intensity of our anger will also diminish. It doesn't mean that we should hold back and repress all feelings of anger, but simply that we should change the orientation of our mind. Emotions are like waves and they always calm down. Whenever we become conscious that we're getting angry, we should try to divert our attention to something else that can take the place of our angry feelings.

There are a great many techniques designed to help deal with and transform negative emotions. Buddhism is in fact mainly centered on such techniques, which we will go into in detail later.

There are three different levels in dealing with emotions: the path of the shravakas, that of the Mahayana, and the tantric path.

The vehicle of the shravakas teaches the antidote: the way to deal with a negative emotion is to think of the opposite emotion. When we feel angry, we think of something that generates love and compassion, which replace anger. We don't suppress anger, we just try to feel love and compassion instead of anger. There is suppression when we're filled with anger but don't express it, whereas here, it's completely different: we forget about the anger and think only of love and compassion. Anger is no longer present. It's like heating a room so that the cold disappears. We don't "repress" the cold; we simply heat the room. That's the way of the shravakas, the general Buddhist path, the first stage.

The second method for dealing with one's emotions is that of the Mahayana, which consists in understanding shunyata along with the previous method. In other words, if we understand the true nature of anger, the real nature of the mind, when anger appears, all we have to do is contemplate that there is no one to irritate us, no one getting angry, and no anger inside us existing independently. To arrive at this understanding, there are two techniques: analysis and meditation. We can approach the emotion by analyzing it intellectually, or we can contemplate it through meditation: we let anger invade us and we look at it. We'll then discover that anger doesn't exist independently. In both cases, anger disappears. More precisely, we discover that there is no one thing that we can isolate as "I" or "anger." The anger disappears through our understanding, our realization of the true nature of phenomena and of our mind. That's the way of Madhyamika,[13] the way of the bodhisattvas.

Finally there is the tantric method of the Vajrayana, which is the total acceptance of anger as it manifests. We see the anger arising and we let it come without fighting it back. We then relax into the anger, which disappears by itself. It can no longer affect us because we have no negative feeling toward it. We're neither for it nor against it: we are conscious of its presence but not attached to it. We simply let ourselves relax in this anger, which dissolves of its own accord and transforms into wisdom. We speak in this case of "liberation (from emotion) through wisdom."

These are the three Buddhist methods for controlling emotions. Try to use all the three methods either in this or in random order.

The Signs and Benefits of Having Developed Loving-Kindness

Through this training, we gradually learn to live without feelings of hatred even toward our enemies. We progressively develop more and more loving-kindness. The texts say that love can be considered to be genuine when tears come to our eyes and we have gooseflesh when we think of sentient beings' sufferings. If that's what we feel for all other beings, we can speak of infinite love and compassion. If we're no longer concerned with our own personal interest but our only concern is the well-being of others, then we have perfectly developed loving-kindness.

This practice enables one to accumulate the greatest merits. Gampopa quotes *The Garland of Jewels*:[14] "The merit of giving, three times a day, every day, three hundred meals fit for a king cannot even begin to compare with that created by a single instant of loving-kindness." Gampopa also mentions the eight positive effects of cultivating loving-kindness, listed in the same sutra: to be loved by gods and humans, to be protected by gods and humans, to have a joyous mind, to encounter pleasant circumstances, not to be the victim of poisoning, not to be wounded by weapons, to be able to achieve most of one's aspirations, and, finally, to be born in the divine realms. These eight results endure until we are definitively liberated from samsara.

There are many stories that illustrate the positive effects of meditating on love and compassion. One of these is about a very powerful evil spirit that once visited the camp of a lama. He walked up and down the camp and no one even saw him. "All these lamas are quite useless," he thought. "I can do any harm I like to any of them." He went straight to the tent of the highest lama. He saw a little old person sitting in a meditation box. He went in and sat on the head of this lama, thinking that he would crush him. But the old lama did not resist. Instead, he started to become flat, and then he started to laugh. He shrank but never stopped laughing. The evil spirit suddenly felt very sad. The more the old lama laughed, the sadder the spirit felt. He started to cry and could not stop. He cried his heart out and left. For more than a year he was unable to hurt anybody; he couldn't even think about it. The old lama had been meditating on love and compassion.

Meditating on loving-kindness protects us like an armor from all negative influence. Even better, this meditation allows us to help and be helped. When we feel well cared for, helped by what we could call positive energies, it isn't some external "energy" but our own loving-kindness that does the work. Healing through love is an effective traditional method!

THE DEVELOPMENT OF COMPASSION[15]

The second aspect of the third antidote is the development of compassion.

Compassion is the heart, the essence of all Buddhist teachings. If you understand what compassion is and practice it, you practice Buddhism. Without compassion, you're not practicing Buddhism.

The Buddha also said that if you have compassion, you possess all the teachings and practices of Buddha. If you lack compassion, you've understood nothing at all.

Just as we distinguished three forms of love, there are also three forms of compassion:

1. With reference to sentient beings,
2. With reference to the Dharma, and
3. Without reference point.

The first type of compassion awakens in us when we see the misery, problems, and sufferings of other beings. We are moved, touched, and we feel the desire to help them get out of their misery. We want to do something for them.

The second type of compassion marks an increase in our own level of understanding. The first stage is very emotional, and we ourselves suffer at the sight of the misery of others. To access the second level of compassion shows that our understanding of Dharma and of the Four Noble Truths—and therefore our compassion—is deeper.

The third type of compassion comes with the total understanding, the perfect realization of the true nature of things, of shunyata. We then see clearly that those beings who suffer so much have in fact no need to suffer. They suffer because they are confused, because they think and see things in an erroneous way. If they could just look at things differently, without conceptualizing, they could be free of all suffering. Compassion becomes very vivid when we see that the sufferings, although clearly omnipresent, are in fact baseless and so easy to eliminate. What separates beings from liberation is such a thin partition! And yet, by ignorance, by misunderstanding the true nature of things, they suffer intensely and perfectly needlessly. Having gone to the other side ourselves, we see the waste, which causes a great compassion to spontaneously arise in us. Simultaneously, we lose any reference point by understanding that the beings who suffer don't exist in any real, solid, substantial way. Of course, at a relative level—that is to say, from their own point of view—they do suffer greatly. The union of wisdom and compassion arises out of the realization of the true nature of things. This is the very heart of the Buddha: compassion without reference.

This last type of compassion is the objective of the two previous ones, but, of course, to start with, we must develop compassion with reference to sentient beings.

The method that allows us to develop compassion is identical to that used for developing loving-kindness. We visualize our mother and imagine her undergoing great suffering. Imagine her being tortured: what would be the intensity of our compassion! Now other beings, like those reborn in hell, continuously suffer such incredible tortures! According to our tradition, we think of our mother, but you can visualize in her place the person for whom you feel the greatest love and imagine how much you love him or her, how you couldn't stand it if anything bad happened to that person. Having developed this strong feeling, you try to extend it to other beings, aware that you once had with all other beings the same relationship that you now have with this person. We've wandered in samsara for such a long time that all beings have at some point been our mothers, our close relatives, or our friends. All these beings have had the same love and kindness for us as the love and kindness that our mother has extended to us in this life. It's therefore normal to feel for them the same love, the same gratitude, and the same compassion that we feel for our mother in this life. The basic idea is that, if we can love one person very strongly, we can develop the same feeling for two, ten, or a thousand people or more. First we develop benevolence and compassion for those who are close to us, and then we extend these feelings to those to whom we are indifferent, and finally include our enemies.

Instead of imagining our mother or someone who is dear to us, we can also imagine what we would experience if we ourselves had to endure the unbearable tortures of the different infernal realms, and in this way develop a great compassion for all the beings who suffer likewise. All sentient beings seek happiness, well-being, peace, and security, but through ignorance they do the exact opposite of what would ensure the enduring happiness they seek. They accumulate bad karma and acquire again and again the causes of subsequent sufferings—like blind men in the middle of a burning desert, walking around in circles, not knowing how to get out. We aspire to happiness and we fear suffering, and other beings are no different from us on this point. When we recognize this evidence, we naturally wish to help them.

The more we develop compassion, the more natural it becomes. When one meditates deeply and constantly on compassion, one comes to a stage where one *is* compassion, and all selfishness, all egotism disappears. This is what we call the full accomplishment of compassion.

Gampopa quotes the *Text Discussing Avalokiteshvara's Realization,* which says: "If there were one thing that could be placed in the palm of one's hand (to represent) all the Buddha's qualities, what would it be? Great compassion!" He also quotes the *Secret Sutra of the Tathagatas,*[16] which says: "The all-knowing primordial essence-wisdom is rooted in compassion."

If you have developed the love that wishes happiness for all beings, and the compassion that urges you to liberate all from suffering, you can no longer care for your own liberation only and, automatically, whether you wanted to or not, you have in fact become a bodhisattva.

In order to become a completely enlightened buddha, you need first of all to have become a bodhisattva. The development of loving-kindness and compassion is therefore the true, direct path to enlightenment.

Even on a relative level, having a heart full of loving-kindness and compassion can help us solve our temporary problems. If we're only benevolent and compassionate, how could we possibly have psychological or mental problems? Such problems are born from selfishness, from attachment to one's self and the consequent fear. Without attachment there is no fear, and without fear there are no problems!

Tolerance could be a first step toward compassion. Tolerance means forgiving, not bearing grudges, striving to understand more deeply the motivations of others, and not returning evil with evil, a basic attitude from which compassion can spring. Compassion is trying to solve problems on this basis. This means that if somebody wants to harm you, you don't answer hate with hate and, on top of it, you wish to help your adversaries to get rid of their hatred and its causes.

However, one shouldn't confuse tolerance with passivity. Tolerance doesn't mean putting up with everything, allowing oneself to be exploited and beaten up. We should be compassionate and do what is good for others—and ourselves. There are also certain things toward which we shouldn't be tolerant, for example, mental poisons. Tolerance isn't applicable to our own anger: we shouldn't allow it to grow and overpower us. Tolerance isn't applicable to those who kill and oppress other people, and we shouldn't let them do it. One shouldn't resort to violence, to arms or conflict, but neither should we accept everything passively. We should defend firmly what we consider just, but avoid harming others as much as possible.

FOURTH ANTIDOTE

Bodhichitta

We could define Gampopa's book as a manual for attaining buddhahood, which is the most accomplished form of nirvana. To achieve it, bodhichitta is indispensable. Bodhichitta is the vow, the great aspiration to attain buddhahood for the benefit of all beings. It is the wish to bring all beings to complete happiness, to the cessation of all suffering, to enlightenment, to buddhahood.

Gampopa quotes *The Ornament of Perfect Realization*,[17] one of the five treatises transmitted by Maitreya to Asanga, which says: "Developing bodhichitta means longing for true, perfect enlightenment in order to benefit others." *Bodhi* means "buddha mind," or "understanding, knowledge, realization." *Chitta* means "mind." *Bodhichitta* therefore means "mind of bodhi," "mind set on realization." The buddha mind, the bodhi, shows aspects of both wisdom and compassion. To become a buddha it is necessary to develop wisdom and compassion simultaneously. Bodhichitta encompasses both aspects.

We distinguish two types of bodhichitta: ultimate bodhichitta[18] and relative bodhichitta.[19] Ultimate bodhichitta corresponds to the wisdom aspect, while the compassion aspect is at the heart of relative bodhichitta.

Ultimate Bodhichitta

Ultimate bodhichitta is the realization of truth, of the ultimate nature, of the ultimate reality. It is buddha nature, the enlightened mind, which encompasses and pervades all phenomena. Gampopa defines ultimate bodhichitta as "voidness with compassion as its essence, clear and unwavering, free from all speculative extremes." This is also how it is presented in the sutras.

A bodhisattva experiences it for the first time when upon reaching the first bhumi. It is actually this very experience that marks one's entrance into this first bhumi.

Ultimate bodhichitta arises from understanding and meditation on the right view. The intellectual understanding of the right view usually happens long before the first bhumi, the level at which, through the first flash of absolute bodhichitta, we experience the true nature of our mind and of phenomena (as phenomena are all perceived by mind). However, we should know that intellectual understanding—although necessary and useful—is not sufficient and should be integrated into our experience so as to become true realization.

The more clearly we perceive it, the more we progress from bhumi to bhumi, to attain finally the last level, the tenth bhumi, which is that of complete realization. All the veils of confusion are then lifted: that is buddhahood. Our progress on the bodhisattva path can therefore be measured by the degree of clarity with which we perceive the true nature of our mind.

The insight into ultimate bodhichitta is not the fruit of taking vows, and we cannot get it through somebody else's blessings. We cannot say either that it is the direct result of study, reflection, and practice, but we can clear the way for its emergence through what we could call the three ways of generating ultimate bodhichitta. First of all, there is study, the deep understanding that one can gain through studying the teachings of the Buddha. Then there is the accumulation of great merit and great wisdom. Finally, there is the realization of wisdom by the development, and then the emergence, of perfectly pure, nonconceptual wisdom. Bodhichitta can sometimes develop through the inspiration we receive from our spiritual guide, if we have such a guide. It can also develop by the power of our natural compassion. Certain methods are more stable than others. Bodhichitta arising from inspiration is less stable than bodhichitta generated by performing good actions, reflecting on the teachings, acquiring a better understanding of bodhichitta, and taking meditation and practice as a way of life, which are the best ways of developing it.

Relative Bodhichitta

Relative bodhichitta has two levels: (1) the bodhichitta of aspiration and (2) the bodhichitta of commitment.

On this subject, there is a slight difference between the view of Nagarjuna and that of Asanga. According to Nagarjuna's definition, which Shantideva and Gampopa endorse, the difference between these two kinds of bodhichitta is the same as that between saying, "I want to go to Paris" and actually going there.

The bodhichitta of aspiration is when we think, "The infinite number of beings who inhabit the universe to the very end of space all desire total happiness and loathe suffering. However, as long as they remain in confusion and ignorance, they will continue to suffer. The only state that is free of all suffering is perfect enlightenment." We then commit ourselves to attain enlightenment for the benefit of all beings, so that we can free them from suffering. Such a vow, combined with the deep desire to realize it, is the bodhichitta of aspiration.

Taking steps to make this wish come true—for example, by taking vows and observing them, by starting up a charity, by trying to be more tolerant, or by following a program of meditation or study—everything which helps us to realize our aspiration is, according to Shantideva, the bodhichitta of commitment. On this subject, he says:

> *Just as one knows the difference between wanting to go and*
>   *actually going,*
> *So the sage should distinguish between these two respectively.*

According to Asanga, promising to obtain a result is the bodhichitta of aspiration, whereas committing oneself to put into action the means to bring this about, harnessing oneself to the cause, is commitment bodhichitta. In other words, saying, "I want to become a buddha for the benefit of all beings" corresponds to the bodhichitta of aspiration: our objective is clear, but we have so far done nothing to attain it. If we add, "To realize this objective, I am going to practice the six paramitas," then it becomes the bodhichitta of commitment.

The causes that help us develop relative bodhichitta are: (1) having a good spiritual guide who inspires us and (2) the impetus of our karma, by which we feel natural compassion. This positive karma is the result of a great accumulation of merit and wisdom gained through different practices, study, and meditation.

The causes that help us generate ultimate bodhichitta are threefold:

1. A deep understanding of the teachings of the Buddha,
2. A great accumulation of merit and wisdom, and
3. The realization of primordial, nonconceptual wisdom.

THE BODHICHITTA OF ASPIRATION

Refuge

In the tradition of Atisha Dipankara, followed by Gampopa, it is considered that one must have previously taken refuge or one of the Vinaya vows[20] to be capable of developing true bodhichitta. Indeed, we may well wish that all beings escape from their suffering and attain total liberation, but we don't know how to go about it. Without a model, without a path, we're at a loss. To know how and where we should begin, we need the help of someone who knows and who has the capacity to transmit this knowledge. Adopting this strategy is what is known as taking refuge.

We can take refuge in many things. If we have nowhere to sleep, a house will be our refuge. If it's raining, we will take refuge in a shelter. If we're hungry, we will find refuge in a restaurant. A refuge is what satisfies a specific need. In the particular case we are dealing with, we seek refuge in order to escape from the sufferings of samsara. We've understood that there's no lasting happiness anywhere in the samsaric realms, and we want to leave samsara behind forever, but we need to know how. If this is our aim, whatever allows us to realize it will be our refuge. In whom we take refuge must have the power, the knowledge, the will, and the compassion necessary to protect us from suffering and show us the way out. Only the Buddha (our aim), the Dharma (the teachings), and the Sangha (our guides) fulfill these criteria. This is why every Buddhist traditionally takes refuge in the Buddha, the Dharma, and the Sangha, which we call the Three Jewels. Taking refuge is not just asking the Buddha, Dharma, and Sangha to help and save us. It means finding a purpose and a path and committing ourselves in that direction.

Taking Refuge in the Buddha

According to the Mahayana, the true refuge is the Buddha.

Prince Siddhartha liberated himself from the sufferings of samsara by becoming a buddha twenty-five hundred years ago. He became the model, the ideal for all of us. He showed us the goal, the true objective: we all have buddha nature in us, we all have buddha potential, which we have to recognize and realize. To accept this means we try to follow the stages on the path, in order to realize our potential for enlightenment. This is the most important element in refuge.

Prince Siddhartha became a buddha by his own efforts, his own understanding of the teachings, and through the example of the other buddhas who came before him. He declared: "I am liberated from the sufferings of samsara, and I know the path that leads to liberation. Anyone who wants to can also become a buddha."

Expounding the Four Noble Truths, he explained very clearly how and why we are subject to the sufferings of samsara (First Noble Truth, the Truth of Suffering). He explained the origins of this suffering (Second Noble Truth, the Truth of the Origins of Suffering) and declared that it is possible to liberate oneself from it (Third Noble Truth, the Truth of Cessation). He then outlined the progressive path we can follow in order to leave samsara behind (Fourth Noble Truth, the Truth of the Path). He gave us not only the "manual" to understand the sufferings of this world but also the "map" to get free from it. He is therefore our only model, the only guide with the necessary experience to lead us to the end of the path. We couldn't find anyone more qualified in whom to take refuge. There have been countless buddhas in the past and there will be countless buddhas in the future.

Outside the strictly historical framework, a buddha is someone who has abandoned everything that had to be abandoned and accomplished everything that had to be accomplished. He or she is purified of all confusion and negative emotions. His or her wisdom has completely blossomed. The name "Buddha" comes from the Sanskrit root *bodh*, which means "understanding" or "knowledge." A buddha is therefore one who understands everything that has to be understood. The Tibetan translation is even clearer. *Sang-gye* is composed of *sang*, which means "awakened" or "enlightened," and *gye*, which means "opening, blossoming." *Sang-gye* therefore means one who has awakened from the slumber of ignorance and whose wisdom has completely blossomed.

We consider the Buddha as a model to imitate, an ideal to attain, but we must also understand that buddha nature is present in every sentient being. We each have this potential to become fully enlightened.

It's with this objective that we start on the path. The essential element in refuge is this recognition of the possibility we have to become completely enlightened beings and the understanding that we share this potential with all beings. To decide to pursue the path of enlightenment in order to help oneself and all sentient beings is what taking refuge in the Buddha means.

Taking Refuge in the Dharma

By taking refuge in the Buddha, we give our lives a meaning, a direction, an objective and a purpose; and by doing this, we automatically take refuge in the Dharma. Indeed, the only way of attaining the level of consciousness of a buddha is to take the Buddha's teachings as a way of life and apply their methods. To decide to learn and practice the Dharma is what taking refuge in the Dharma means.

We distinguish two aspects of the Dharma:

1. Teaching Dharma; the oral teachings of the Buddha and the instructions, the guidance, the methods transmitted by the lineage of his students and
2. Experience Dharma; the "true" Dharma, which includes the "Dharma of the path" (that is, the understanding and the experience of the Dharma) and the "Dharma of cessation" (which corresponds to the moment when we attain the final result of our practice, namely enlightenment).

Taking Refuge in the Sangha

We receive these teachings and these instructions from the Sangha, which is the community of practitioners, our travel companions in the Dharma, those who practice and have received the teachings passed on from one generation to the next. The members of the Sangha are those who give us instructions regarding the Dharma. We wouldn't have access to the Dharma without their help and guidance. They show us the way; they sustain us step by step and warn us so that we may avoid mistakes and pitfalls.

There are also two types of Sangha:

1. The Sangha of ordinary beings, which comprises the communities of fully ordained monks and nuns (*gelong*s or *bhikshu*s) and lay practitioners.
2. The Sangha of bodhisattvas (*arya* Sangha or supreme Sangha) who have the experience of the Dharma. The Buddha is also included in this Sangha, because he has the deepest experience of the Dharma.

We speak of a group Sangha as soon as there are more than four bhikshus or bodhisattvas together.

The importance given to one or another of these aspects of refuge depends on each individual practitioner. Those for whom the intellectual approach is difficult and those who don't have a very independent character and like to follow a group will get better results if they form part of a community of practitioners. The emphasis is then given to the Sangha. By following it, they learn how to practice Dharma, and in the end succeed in understanding the Buddha.

For those who do not want to depend on others and to be part of a group, more emphasis is given to the Dharma, which is then presented as the true refuge, since it is through the Dharma that one realizes the Buddha and that one comes into contact with the inner Sangha.

However, according to Mahayana Buddhism, the main refuge is the Buddha. The *Uttaratantra Shastra*[21] and other central Mahayana texts explain in detail that the Buddha is the only ultimate refuge. They emphasize our potential to become buddhas and urge us to consider the actualization of this potential as our sole aim.

We find a purpose by going for refuge to the Buddha. We find a way by going for refuge to the Dharma, and we create the right circumstances for our practice by going for refuge to the Sangha. Taking refuge in Buddha, Dharma, and Sangha is practicing the spiritual path or the path to Buddhahood.

The Three Kayas

Now we should of course have an idea of what a buddha is, since there is no meaning in wanting to become something we know nothing about!

In a general way, as previously stated, we can define a buddha as a being who has developed his or her wisdom and compassion to the utmost, ultimate level. However, there's no simple definition of what a buddha is, and therefore we have to approach his nature from different angles.

A buddha is thus described as possessing three kayas, or "bodies," which are the dharmakaya, the sambhogakaya, and the nirmanakaya.[22] This notion isn't always very well understood. It doesn't mean that the buddha has different forms, but that what we call "buddha" can be described from three angles, three aspects, or three points of view.

The Dharmakaya The dharmakaya indicates the absence of dualistic thought of the type "This is me and these are the others"; "This is good and this is bad." A buddha is free of such concepts because he has perfectly realized emptiness, or shunyata. Some people think that the absence of dualistic perception implies that all distinction between self and others disappears and that one is then reduced to nothingness, as if one were atomized or had sunk into a deep coma. They then wonder what could possibly be desirable about such a state and come to the conclusion that it's preferable to abandon all spiritual practice and content oneself with pursuing worldly pleasures. They forget that this is not the only aspect that characterizes a buddha.

The dharmakaya is the Buddha's mind. It is completely free from any delusion so it is free from concepts, assumptions, grasping, doubts, and fear. It is limitless, boundless, clear and direct awareness. The thinking mind that we experience is unclear and full of assumptions and inferences. The mind of dharmakaya transcends that and sees directly and clearly, hence there is no need to have concepts or assumptions. This is the deepest experience of the true nature of our mind. The Buddha's mind is omniscient because it is not fettered with dualistic thoughts. This experience is also called *rigpa*, Mahamudra, clear light and Great Perfection. Like space, it is limitless, un-compounded, unable to be grasped and identified in any way. It is always there but you cannot capture it. It is peaceful—nothing can disturb it. It is clear—everything is seen unobstructedly. It is compassionate—all beings are seen as equal to oneself. It is powerful—a dharmakaya being can emanate and arise as anything or anybody, as is needed, with no effort. This is the essential nature of all of our minds.

The Sambhogakaya Sambhogakaya is the way buddhas see themselves: as the radiance of the five wisdoms, ever pure, as it can never be defiled; ever youthful, as it is beyond birth, death, and change. The literary translation of sambhogakaya is "body of enjoyment."

If the dharmakaya is the complete and total realization of what we call "buddha mind" in its original, pure state, free of all duality and negative emotion, the sambhogakaya is the presence of different aspects of wisdom. Buddha nature is not a dull state comparable to deep sleep. On the contrary, it is alive with vibrant and powerful energies, what we call the five wisdoms. To explain it very briefly, the five negative emotions (anger, desire, pride, jealousy, and ignorance) can be transformed into the five corresponding wisdoms. Buddha nature, far from being an empty void, or just clear awareness, also possesses these energies, these wisdoms. This is why the sambhogakaya forms of the buddhas are always represented in Tibetan religious art as young and beautiful princes or princesses, adorned with jewels and magnificent ornaments symbolizing the vivacity, the shining radiance of this aspect of buddhahood.

The Nirmanakaya The third aspect is the nirmanakaya. Nirmanakaya is what is seen by others. When one becomes a buddha, one doesn't disappear from this world like a blown-out candle flame. The flow, the continuity, of the buddha emanations remains and never stops. Just as we experience this life and a succession of rebirths within samsara, when one becomes completely enlightened, buddha mind continues to manifest in all the forms that are necessary and useful for the benefit of beings. A buddha no longer has any limited or egotistical thoughts; he can manifest innumerable emanations, without being restricted by space, time, variety, or number. These manifestations are what we call the nirmanakaya.

The three kayas are one way of describing and understanding the qualities of a buddha. All three aspects are present at the same time. A buddha's mind is absolutely clear and aware and therefore does not need to make any assumptions and concepts because all is perceived directly. It sees the enlightened as well as the unenlightened aspects and can manifest in whatever way that might help beings.

The three kayas are also the inherent nature of our own mind. When we realize them experientially, that is enlightenment.

The Refuge Ceremony

The refuge ceremony formally marks the moment when one becomes a Buddhist. It is about choosing a direction and a path for oneself.

Traditionally, one takes refuge with a lama, but it is also possible to do it in front of an image of a buddha or a bodhisattva. We first make three prostrations to the person with whom we are about to take refuge. The prostrations are the formal request to take refuge. The Buddha forbade any of his followers to give refuge, or for that matter, any precepts or teachings, without being specifically asked. Thereafter, following the teacher, we repeat the refuge prayer three times. That is the refuge ceremony. In the Tibetan system, we usually get a new name to denote that we have started a new way of life. The lama also cuts a little piece of our hair, to represent that we make the highest offering to the Buddha, Dharma, and Sangha. As hair grows on the highest part of the body, this represents a significant offering.

In the course of this ceremony, one makes different vows relating to the three objects of refuge: three principal vows, three vows linked to positive actions, and three vows linked to negative actions. The three general vows are:

1. To be constantly mindful of the Buddha, the Dharma, and the Sangha, whatever we are doing—as we get up, as we eat, wherever we go—and to make mental offerings to them;
2. Never to forsake the refuge of the Three Jewels, not even to obtain great rewards or to avoid great losses; and
3. To repeat the refuge prayer as often as possible and to think of the qualities and benefits of taking refuge.

The three specific vows linked to negative actions are:

1. Not to take "lesser refuges."[23] Our refuge can be nothing less than the completely enlightened Buddha.
2. To avoid any form of violence and to try not to wound or kill any living being. The Dharma is, in essence, nonviolence.
3. To avoid being led into bad company and committing negative actions under the influence of bad friends. That doesn't mean that we can't have a thief, an alcoholic, or a gambler among our friends, but we must avoid being led into imitating their bad behavior, and we should always try to seek the company of people who can be a positive example for us.

The three vows linked to positive actions stress that we must show respect:

1. For enlightened beings and even images and paintings that represent them,
2. For books and documents that represent the Dharma, and
3. For the members of the Sangha, monks and nuns, as well as for all representations of the Three Jewels.

The eight benefits of taking refuge are as follows. One becomes a Buddhist, that is to say, someone who concentrates on his or her inner development.[24] One thus receives the basis for future precepts and developments. One purifies negative karma arising from past negative actions. One is protected against attacks from humans and spirits. One will be capable of accomplishing all one's vows. One accumulates merit all the time as a result of the important goal one has set for oneself. One no longer falls back into the lower realms. Finally, one is on the path toward enlightenment.

THE BODHICHITTA OF COMMITMENT

The Bodhisattva Vows

The bodhichitta of commitment draws its inspiration from the concrete expression of the bodhichitta of aspiration through, for example, taking vows with one's guru or teacher. It's preferable to take vows with a teacher if possible. However, if that's not possible, one can take vows in the absence of a guru in two ways. One can place in front of oneself an image of either a bodhisattva or the Buddha, recalling that a buddha or a bodhisattva is always present when one sincerely thinks of him. If one has no image, one can visualize the buddha or the bodhisattva in the sky above one's head. One then says the formula: "In front of all the buddhas and the bodhisattvas, I take the bodhisattva vows." As soon as we have taken these vows, it is said that everything we do (or don't do) makes us accumulate the merit of a bodhisattva, because we have strongly committed ourselves to becoming one.

This commitment is a token of the greatest compassion, since the vow involves helping not only one, two, ten thousand, or one hundred thousand beings but all sentient beings, everywhere, in every universe. What we wish for them is that they should all, without exception, be freed from even the slightest suffering of samsara. We pray that they may all find the greatest happiness possible, which is enlightenment, buddhahood. We pray that they may enjoy this perfect state not only for a limited time but forever. This is the greatest, highest, and noblest thought that one can conceive of.

According to Asanga's tradition, the vows of the bodhichitta of aspiration and those of the bodhichitta of commitment are taken separately, whereas they are taken simultaneously according to Nagarjuna's tradition.

Usually, the ceremony has three stages: preparation, the taking of the vows, and the conclusion.

The preparation begins with the seven-branch prayer: (1) paying homage, (2) making offerings, (3) purification by confession, (4) rejoicing in the positive acts performed by oneself and others, (5) begging the buddhas and bodhisattvas to teach us, (6) asking all realized beings not to pass away, but to stay among us in the world, and finally (7) dedicating all the positive results one has been able to gather to the complete realization of enlightenment by all beings. The seven-branch prayer is found in nearly all the Tibetan Buddhist *sadhanas*[25] and forms a very important part of the practice. Here it is performed before the taking of the bodhisattva vows to emphasize the importance of the event.

I would like to make three remarks regarding this prayer.

The first concerns the offerings made to the buddhas and bodhisattvas. These offerings are not necessarily real things that we possess. We can also imagine and give as offerings things that we find beautiful and that we desire, even if they do not belong to us. Considering them as offerings, we no longer feel attached to these objects. This is actually an excellent practice, since we no longer desire them for ourselves.

The second remark concerns confession and purification. We must bear in mind that there is nothing that cannot be purified, whatever negative acts we have committed or think we have committed, whatever negative karma we have accumulated (whether we remember or not). In order to purify this bad karma, four elements must be present. We must first of all (1) be able to recognize a negative act: an act that brings suffering and problems for ourselves and others, and (2) feel a sincere regret for any negative act that we ourselves might have done or made others to do knowingly or unknowingly, (3) commit ourselves, as much as possible, to not doing it again, and, having established this train of thought, finally (4) purify ourselves in the presence of the buddhas or the bodhisattvas by doing something positive, including helping others, meditating, reciting mantras, or any other positive action. If we do this sincerely, from the depths of our heart, there is nothing that we cannot purify.

The last remark is about the dedication. This dedication is also essential and should be as broad, as generous, as spacious and without limitations as possible. Among a bodhisattva's skillful means, the two main ones are aspiration and dedication. Every practice must be preceded by the development of aspiration or right motivation. Whatever we do, even if it is only the recitation of a single *mala*[26] of the mantra OM MANI PEME HUNG or a short meditation session, it must be done for the benefit of all beings. It then becomes an event bearing great significance and powerful positive consequences. Likewise, we must close each practice by dedicating it to the benefit of all beings (so that they all may attain enlightenment), which multiplies its effect. It is said that even a very lengthy and comprehensive practice or a magnificent offering dedicated for a precise and specific objective will perhaps lead to the achievement of the result sought for, but no more than that. On the other hand, even a short practice or a modest offering accompanied by a very broad dedication will generate much greater merit. The positive effects will be recurring, that is, they will be felt until the wish expressed in our dedication is accomplished. Our dedication should therefore be as broad, as great, and as ambitious as possible. Any personal or specific wish should be added afterward as a second dedication. This is how a bodhisattva proceeds.

Taking the bodhisattva vows is not a simple event devoid of consequences. This decision will have a great impact on the rest of our lives. If a marriage requires great preparations (since it is supposed to be a commitment for life), the bodhisattva vows constitute an even greater commitment. It is as if we were "marrying" all the beings from every part of space and from all time to come, until we attain enlightenment—which will perhaps take many cosmic ages. It is therefore a tremendously important event for which we must prepare ourselves properly. I think it should be the occasion for a great celebration.

The ceremony itself is very simple. To take bodhisattva vows, one simply has to repeat the following formula three times after the teacher:

Just as the buddhas of the past developed bodhichitta and trained themselves gradually in it, so will I also gradually progress through the bodhisattva training. Having taken the commitment to reach enlightenment in order to benefit sentient beings, I also will train stage by stage in the relevant disciplines.

The important word here is "gradually." One cannot at the beginning resemble a buddha of the tenth bhumi, but one can try to be like him when he started out. Like him, we progress step by step, without unnecessary haste. We are perhaps setting out for hundreds or thousands of lives. We advance steadily, without excess, without tension, but consistently. This is very important. If we are too enthusiastic when we set out, we risk overdoing it; as we are not prepared, disillusionment and discouragement will soon take over. We risk losing sight of our initial aim—that is, to work to relieve the suffering of all beings—and thus abandoning our bodhisattva vows.

It is the same as for generosity. We can give anything we like, as long as we do it freely and with pleasure. At the beginning, we will perhaps be capable of giving only a glass of water without regret, without a feeling of sacrifice, spontaneously and joyfully. When generosity grows, it becomes easy to give even something of great value. In the end, we will perhaps even be capable of giving our own life, because we will feel no more attachment for our body than we did for the glass of water at the beginning.

A sad story illustrates the danger of doing too much too quickly. A long time ago there lived a bodhisattva of great diligence who wanted to progress as rapidly as possible. He announced publicly that he would give away anything that anyone asked him for. So some came for money, others for food. He was very rich. One day, a rather disagreeable beggar came and asked him, "Is it true that you are ready to give away anything that people ask you for?" The bodhisattva replied, "Yes, I give freely everything I have, whatever you ask for." The beggar then said to him, "Give me your right hand." The bodhisattva took a knife, cut off his hand, and gave it to the beggar. The beggar then said, "I could never accept something given with the left hand. This is really improper!" That was too much for the bodhisattva, who cried out, "That's it! I'm not giving anything else to anyone! I'm not a bodhisattva any more! Get out!" and with that he abandoned the bodhisattva path.

The taking of bodhisattva vows is followed by an offering of gratitude to the teacher and closes with a last celebration. We rejoice in having accomplished something great and positive. Regarding this gratitude offering, those who are rich can make great offerings, while those who possess nothing may offer nothing. In the stories of the lives of the previous buddhas, we read that some offered millions of gold coins when they took bodhisattva vows for the first time, whereas others offered only a blade of grass. It's not the material value of the offering that counts but the state of mind in which it is made, the purity of the motivation.

Instructions for Developing the Bodhichitta of Commitment: The Six Paramitas

We come now to the precepts of the bodhichitta of commitment. We can summarize all the bodhisattva practices in three words:

1. Morality (ethical conduct),[27]
2. Meditation,[28] and
3. Wisdom.[29]

These three trainings are none other than the six paramitas, which can be considered the bodhisattvas' precepts, how they should try to act and live. Literally, *paramita* means "to go beyond," "to transcend."[30] Practicing the six paramitas allows us to overcome our mental poisons, to transcend all concepts, and to see the true nature of things. They are the methods through which we can reach enlightenment.

The first four paramitas—generosity, right conduct, forbearance, and diligence—relate to right living. The fifth is none other than meditation; the sixth, wisdom. The six paramitas are at the heart of all the actions of a bodhisattva, of someone who is training to truly work for others.

The practice of the first three paramitas ensures for us a happy life in samsara. We could say that, if we must remain in samsara anyway, we might as well be rich rather than poor, and only generosity, the cultivation of the art of giving, can bring us that kind of prosperity. Following the same logic, it's better to be in good health than to be sick, which implies respect for moral conduct, since it is said that those who have an ethical lifestyle will enjoy good health. In the same way, if we want to live in an agreeable environment and have good relations with those around us, we must develop forbearance.

The three paramitas that follow help us on the other hand to escape from samsara. Diligence is necessary to develop all the qualities that are within us. Meditation is also an indispensable tool, and meditation leads us to wisdom, which is the sixth paramita.

If we train in the six paramitas, we will have prosperity in this life and all the necessary conditions to liberate ourselves from the sufferings of samsara.

Notice that the six paramitas are presented in the logical order of our progression on the path of the bodhisattva. We begin with the practice of giving, which allows us to become less self-centered and less envious. As soon as we are less possessive—toward things as well as toward people—it is easier to adopt a moral way of life, since the basis of right conduct is nonattachment. In the same way, ethical conduct is the foundation of forbearance. Indeed, forbearance and tolerance develop from self-discipline. Once one is patient, it is easy to develop diligence, because diligence is none other than the capacity to apply oneself intelligently, to uphold one's interest in everything one does, including one's spiritual practice. Meditation then presents no further problems, since diligence has taught us concentration. As for meditation, it makes our mind calm and stable and protects it from distraction and confusion. It is on this ground that wisdom progressively manifests. Indeed, a mind that is perfectly calm and clear sees without difficulty the true nature of phenomena. We could therefore compare the six paramitas to a staircase to enlightenment. Just like steps, each paramita is a support for the next. That is why we are advised, for the sake of ease and speed, to practice them in the right order.

There's a difference between the qualities termed "ordinary" and those termed "transcendent." Take the example of giving. Generosity is always positive, but it only becomes a paramita, only becomes transcendent, when it is accompanied by the wisdom that perceives the insubstantial nature of the giver, what is given and the receiver. The transcendence of the act of giving implies that the giver is attached neither to his or her image, nor to the recipient, nor to what is given. If we give without attachment, we expect nothing in return. Generosity then becomes the paramita of giving. When we are no longer personally and emotionally involved in what we are doing, the mental poisons no longer taint our actions, which then become paramitas.

First Paramita: Generosity[31]

The essence of generosity is nonattachment. Giving enriches us, whereas holding on to things impoverishes us. Such is the karmic process coming into play in the practice of generosity. Few people these days would follow such a reasoning, and yet giving is the true source of prosperity and riches, whereas the result of avarice is poverty.

It is not always obvious, but it is certain that we are never happier than when we have few attachments, when we do not grasp at people and things. Of all possessions, the highest and noblest is contentment. Satisfaction gives us all the riches in the world, since we desire no more than what we have. A contented person is a wealthy person.

This view is not widespread today, and I often hear people say that contented people lack ambition and that without ambition one is nothing. And yet, to me, ambition seems to be a source of stress, and grasping people seem to encounter lots of problems. Of course, modern society is to a large extent built on grasping, on desire. People always want more. Their desire is like a fire that they have to keep burning. Everything they throw onto it is immediately consumed, and they constantly have to find more fuel. The only way to stop it is to find contentment. Desire and grasping are like a bottomless well: you can never fill it. Only contentment will bring us peace. As long as we are not satisfied, we are always running after something, incapable of staying still. Contentment is the prerequisite of a peaceful mind. That in no way means that we shouldn't work or that we should just be satisfied with anything whatsoever. What matters is our attitude toward things. If we remain grasping, racked with an unquenchable thirst, we will never find contentment. We will never be able to enjoy what we have, and we will always want more.

Moreover, if we are particularly grasping and possessive, we risk being reborn in the realm of the hungry ghosts. A hungry ghost is a being who, although he already has lots of things, is convinced that everything else ought to belong to him too. According to the Tibetan tradition, a hungry ghost is like a ball of fire who never manages to touch the things he is trying to eat, and so is never able to taste anything. A hungry ghost sometimes has a belly as big as a barrel, with a narrow neck and a mouth as tiny as the eye of a needle. He doesn't manage to get anything that he's trying to eat into his mouth, and when food nevertheless somehow gets in, his throat is too narrow for the food to get down to his stomach.

According to the Buddha, if we're rich in this life, it is because we've been generous in previous lives. If we want to become rich in the future, we must learn to give now.

A little while ago, I read an interesting book written by an American author whose name I forget. Its title was something like *How to Get Rich Quick*. The author explained that, as a consultant to large firms for whom he trained administrators, he had tried to understand how some men had managed to become so rich. According to him, the only way to get rich quick was to adopt the policies of General Motors in the United States, whose motto is "Give people more of what they want and less of what they don't want." Curiously, this is more or less what is said in the Buddhist tradition, and it echoes our belief that if we give, we will become rich. Of course, the motivation is completely different, but the parallel remains interesting.

If we give more, we'll receive more, perhaps in this life, perhaps in another. If we are rich but don't have the courage to enjoy what we have and share it with others, then no matter how much we possess, it's as if we had nothing. Wealth brings us a certain power, a certain importance, but also many problems, stresses, and worries. I'm not saying that we must lack what is necessary for living; we obviously need money and shouldn't underestimate its importance, but let's remember that there is also a "return," a "dividend" linked to what we give. According to the law of karma, the more we give, the more we receive. However, paradoxically, if we give in order to get something in return, this process no longer functions.

Gampopa quotes many texts that explain what generosity is and what its advantages are. To summarize, we could compare the act of giving to an investment with a very high interest rate. Not only do we get back the sum we initially invested but we also receive considerable interest. By helping others, we improve our own situation, which allows us to give even more in the future, and our generosity grows continuously.

In his *Letter to a Friend*, Nagarjuna says:

> *Knowing that possessions are ephemeral and devoid of essence,*
> *Practice generosity with respect*
> *Toward monks, Brahmans, the destitute, and friends.*
> *For the next life, there is no better friend than what one has given.*

What we've given remains, while what we've kept no longer belongs to us. At the moment of death, everything that we've given becomes essential, whereas what we've kept becomes useless. We're no longer afraid to lose what we've given away, while what we have is a source of anxiety. What we've given away shows us the way to enlightenment, while what we've kept shows us the way of suffering and affliction.

Nonattachment is at the heart of generosity. Generosity is chiefly a state of mind characterized by nonattachment. How generous we are is an indication of how detached we are from what we have.

Three types of giving can be practiced:

1. The giving of material things,
2. The giving of protection, and
3. The giving of the Dharma.

Material things can be given in a pure or an impure fashion. The gift is impure when it is accompanied by a wrong motivation, when one gives things that are inappropriate, when one gives to an inappropriate person, or when one gives in an unskillful way. These four ways of giving do not generate any benefit.

To give with a wrong motivation means to give with the intention to harm, or for one's own glory, or to besmirch a rival.

Things that are inappropriate to give are, for example, poison or weapons that will certainly harm the recipient as much as the person against whom they will be used.

To give to the wrong people is to give to those who have wrong intentions. If a person with wrong motivation or a madman asks us for something that he shouldn't have, or if someone asks for our help to commit suicide, we absolutely must not give what is asked for, since it would only harm the person.

The wrong way to give is to give without joy, without respect, with anger, with hatred, or in an offensive manner. To give away something that our family doesn't want us to give, or that could affect them negatively, is also wrong. In such a case, it's better to abstain.

The four pure ways of giving are exactly the opposite of these ways.

The second type of giving consists in protecting someone from a fear or a danger. The help can be psychological, physical, or material.

The last type of giving, that of the Dharma, consists in pointing out the correct path, what should be done and not done.

There is a difference between the simple fact of giving and the paramita, the transcendence of generosity. To qualify as a paramita, generosity doesn't depend on the size of the gift. Everything lies in the manner of giving, in our detachment and in the way we manage our emotional reactions linked to giving: our avarice, our possessiveness, the image we have of ourselves and our attitude toward the person who receives our gift. We speak of transcendent generosity when we're totally detached from the notion of a giver, a receiver, and what is given, when we cast aside all strategy in giving.

When we give, we must always be mindful of using the "three skillful means of a bodhisattva," which increase the effects of generosity. These are wisdom (*yeshe*), intelligence (*sherab*),[32] and dedication.

To give with wisdom is to be able to view the person who gives (this can be ourselves), the object of the gift, and the person who receives it as dependently arising aggregates like a mirage, a rainbow, or a river. The presence of this understanding transcends the act of giving from samsaric to enlightened and increases its beneficial effects. When we consider subject, act, and object with wisdom, our generosity no longer awakens in us the least attachment or pride. Free from pride and attachment, giving is perfectly pure.

Intelligence encourages us to give with good intentions, in a clever manner. We purify the giving by thinking, "I am making this gift in order that all beings be liberated from suffering and attain enlightenment." This positive motivation frees us from all attachment, from all expectation or hope of reward.

The third skillful means is dedication. We multiply the value of what we give by dedicating the act. Every time we are generous, however small the gift, we should think, "I offer all the merit generated by this act to all beings, that they may attain enlightenment." Traditionally, it is said that, dedicated in this way, the merit generated even by the smallest gift is multiplied by as many times as there are beings in the universe.

With these three skillful means, it doesn't matter whether our gifts are great or small. In both cases they will bring infinite benefit.

Second Paramita: Ethics or Right Conduct[33]

To follow a moral code, to have a right way of living, means to abstain from doing what is negative and to act in a positive way. To develop a way of life that is good for us and can help others is the basis of the other virtues, the foundation of subsequent spiritual development. Without discipline and right conduct, we won't go very far. If we fail to abstain from committing negative deeds and don't live in a positive way, our lives will be neither agreeable nor pleasant but, on the contrary, troubled, perturbed, and tense. We'll lack the conditions necessary for our spiritual development and for the stabilization of our meditation.

Gampopa distinguishes three aspects of right conduct:

1. Acts we must abstain from. This is the ethic of abstention, of observance, the restrictions that correspond to the precepts of the Vinaya and to the vows of Pratimoksha.[34] They group together different levels such as the five precepts of lay disciples (*upasaka* and *upasika*), the vows of novices (*shramanera*) and of fully ordained monks and nuns (bhikshus and *bhikshunis*). From the point of view of the Vinaya, discipline is focused on actions performed with body and speech. The rules are very precise as to what we can or cannot do, what we can or cannot say. These vows prevent us from taking a wrong direction.

2. Positive actions that favor the development of bodhichitta, that is, our compassion and our wisdom. This is called in Tibetan "the discipline that allows us to acquire what is good and positive." This accumulation of positive actions encompasses study, meditation, rejoicing in the happiness of others, encouraging them to perform positive actions, making offerings, practicing the six paramitas, and so on—in short, all that will develop our practice as bodhisattvas. The precepts at this level mainly take into account the state of mind with which an action is accomplished, the underlying intention and motivation. What can and cannot be done is therefore not precisely listed. Thus a seemingly bad action can in fact be motivated by an altruistic intention and will be defined as good at this level, whereas it would be condemned at

the Vinaya level. On the other hand, an apparently good action can be hypocritical and in fact motivated by bad intentions and would be considered a negative deed at this level of conduct.

3. Work for the benefit of others, of which there are thirteen types: (1) helping those who perform beneficial activities, (2) alleviating the sufferings of all beings, (3) instructing those who are ignorant, (4) being grateful and returning favors one has received, (5) protecting those who are afraid, (6) relieving the pain of those who suffer, (7) giving what they lack to those who are in need, (8) rejoicing in virtuous actions, (9) correctly accomplishing one's spiritual practice, (10) helping others to develop their potential and find contentment, (11) eliminating what needs eliminating, (12) inspiring respect by one's talents, and (13) motivating people to aspire to what is good and beneficial. These thirteen points are generally further classified into four groups. The first comprises the activities that put into practice the paramita of generosity. Giving material assistance, protection, or teachings is the first way to help people. The second comprises beneficial advice and clear, comprehensible explanations, which draw people in the right direction, toward the Dharma. The third point underlines the importance of practicing what one teaches. Everything that one says or teaches is useless and can even be harmful if there is no coherence between one's principles and practice. Finally, the last point insists on the necessity, whatever our own level, of placing ourselves at the level of the people we are helping. We must give them what they need, insofar as it is not in conflict with our vows.

Third Paramita: Forbearance[35]

The Tibetan word *zopa* means forbearance, patience, and tolerance. Forbearance is considered one of the most important paramitas, since it is the antidote to one of the most common categories of mind poisons: anger and hatred. Even if we have been practicing generosity and discipline for a long time, a fit of violent anger or hatred can considerably affect our accumulation of good actions, to the point of destroying all their merit. According to the Buddha, nothing is worse than hatred and nothing stronger or better than forbearance. This is why forbearance is such an important practice on the bodhisattva path.

There are three kinds of forbearance. The first consists in not returning evil for evil when confronted with people who do us wrong. The second is forbearance in the face of setbacks and difficult circumstances in life. The third is the courage to face and accept the profound teachings on emptiness, the openness or broad-minded attitude necessary to make the effort to understand them and the patience of not rejecting them if we don't understand them at first.

How can we develop sufficient forbearance not to hate someone who mistreats us? We must change our attitude. When we reason and analyze the situation, different arguments can help us to do this.

The first argument is that such people have probably lost control over themselves. Various causes and circumstances probably give them the impression that they have to act as they do. Someone under the influence of anger or hatred is very much like someone under the influence of alcohol. We don't pay too much attention to what a drunk says or does. Likewise, we shouldn't react strongly to an angry person's words or actions.

Besides, as mental phenomena, anger and compassion are interrelated. Buddhism classes these two emotions in the same category. When we are faced with a disagreeable experience, two emotional reactions are possible: either anger or compassion. When someone irritates us, we react with anger. However, if we relate directly to the cause of our irritation (which is the disagreeable impression experienced and associated with it), we'll start feeling compassion instead, because we come to understand that the person who's making us suffer didn't really mean to do so. Logically, what motivates someone to harm us is his or her ignorance, suffering, fears, and anxieties. Without such causes, the person wouldn't have any reason to try to harm us. Instead of blaming the person, let's blame the negative emotions, the malaise, the confusion, and the suffering that are the real causes of his or her behavior.

Let's rather be angry at the anger than at the person who's only its vehicle. From this perspective, we have many more reasons to feel compassion than to react with hatred or anger toward those who irritate or attack us.

We find a second reason for not reacting with anger when we consider the karmic mechanism involved in any particular situation. If we understand the law of karma, we can better accept negative circumstances arising in our lives, even when they are quite painful, because we understand that what happens to us is the result of similar actions we did in a previous life. In one of our past lives, we must have harmed that person who now causes us problems or wishes us ill. Our suffering is the result of our own karma. Why then get angry at someone if he or she is only the instrument of our own karma? If we react with anger, we only accumulate more bad karma, which will multiply similar situations we'll encounter in the future. On the other hand, if we cultivate forbearance, our negative karma dissolves. It's therefore much wiser not to get angry. Forbearance helps everyone involved and transforms our negative karma into positive karma.

The third argument is that the drawbacks of a situation aren't just attributable to the person who seems to be the cause. Suppose someone throws a stone at us. Why get angry with the person who throws the stone and not with the stone? We could just as well get angry with our own mind and body! Indeed, without body and mind, we would feel no suffering. All of these elements combine to make us experience suffering: our mind, our body, the stone, and the person who threw it, as well as his anger and anguish. Why get angry only at the last one?

A fourth reason not to give in to anger is to understand that, far from harming us, that person is actually helping us. He or she is giving us the opportunity to practice forbearance and therefore to purify our negative karma. This gradual purification will in the end allow us to attain enlightenment! The apparent ill will of that person in fact gives us a precious opportunity to train; and instead of resenting him or her, we should on the contrary be grateful.

When the Buddha gave his first teachings at Sarnath, the first disciple who understood them and became an arhat was Kondiniya. When other disciples asked why, the Buddha told them the following story:

A long time ago, in one of my previous lives, I was a rishi, a hermit, whose name was Kshantivadin ("He Who Loves to Be Patient"). I spent my life in meditation in a very beautiful clearing in the forest. One day, a very powerful king came to picnic there with all his queens, his ministers, and his retinue. The king went off to hunt and the queens started to pick fruit and flowers. They came upon the clearing where I was meditating, gave me some offerings, and sat down around me to listen to me. When the king came back from hunting, he found the tents empty. All his wives had disappeared! He went looking for them and found them sitting around me. The king got very angry, thinking, "Who's this man who monopolizes the attention of all my wives?" He shouted at me, "What are you doing? What's your name? Why are you stealing my wives?" I replied, "I've done nothing; they came to me spontaneously. My name is Kshantivadin, The One Who Loves to Be Patient." At these words, the king's anger intensified. "Ah, ah! You're patient? We'll see how far!" He took his sword and cut off one of my legs, then asked, "So, you're still forbearing? Aren't you angry with me?" I answered, "No, I'm not, I'm very happy!" The king then cut off my limbs one after the other. I simply said to him, "Not only am I not angry, but I think on the contrary that you're helping me greatly. You're transforming me in such a way that I will become completely enlightened very rapidly. I therefore make the following prayer: when I become a buddha, I wish that you be the first person whose ignorance and confusion are destroyed. In this way, I too will transform you into a totally enlightened being." Many lives later, thanks to this vow, this person became the first of my disciples to attain realization.

Another argument for not reacting with anger has us examine why we react with anger. What exactly are we looking for? Do we wish to make the other unhappy, to make him suffer? If this is the case, what would be the worst we could do to him? Kill him? If this is what we're after, all we are doing is advancing the hour of his death a little. He'll have to die one day anyway! When we kill someone, we bear the bad karma associated with this act. If we don't kill him, he will die of his own accord. With forbearance, we are the winners. Furthermore, if we want him to suffer in his turn, have no doubt, he will! He's the one who will have to bear all the bad karma associated with his action. Even now, the hatred or the anger he feels throws him into a state of discomfort. Hatred and anger burn you inside and bring you great suffering. Forbearance is thus a much wiser method.

When we examine the main cause of anger and hatred—feeling hurt or threatened by someone—we see that harboring anger until it becomes hatred does not ease the hurt. Holding on to hatred also hurts, so it's better to forgive.

These are some of the numerous arguments that can help us to subdue anger and adopt a patient attitude. An "advanced" bodhisattva no longer needs such logical reasoning since he or she is naturally free from anger, but for us who are still subject to impatience, irritation, anger, and hatred, it is good to recall regularly all the good reasons we have to be forbearing.

The second kind of forbearance is the one we develop to confront the difficult circumstances of life. When we set out on a spiritual path, it's probable that we'll encounter many obstacles. If we're seriously ill, we agree to undergo an operation or a painful treatment because we understand that it's a lesser evil that enables us to avoid a greater one. We must show the same forbearance, the same confidence, to endure the difficulties we encounter on our path when we want to "heal" the sufferings of samsara. Let's behave like valiant warriors. Someone who's capable of confronting a great danger or a ferocious enemy is considered brave and courageous. By committing ourselves to the Dharma, we're actually engaging in a battle with our worst and most powerful enemies: our negative emotions, which have caused us so much suffering and have kept us in the grasp of their tyranny from time immemorial until today. If we manage to crush such enemies, we'll become victors forever! Such an endeavor demands that we be ready for every challenge and every difficulty.

The third kind of forbearance consists in persevering with our studies, listening and learning until we understand the truth. To understand profound teachings demands forbearance. We should be confident that we will understand later what we don't understand now, and persevere in our efforts. To thoroughly understand the deepest aspects of the Buddhist philosophy is something so great, so extraordinary, that we must not expect to achieve it all at once. We must be patient, work harder, show greater interest, and persevere in our meditation, and little by little this understanding will develop. Let's not be impatient, let's not be discouraged, let's not close our mind, thinking that we will never understand the philosophy of emptiness. Absolute bodhichitta, the dharmakaya, emptiness, ultimate truth are difficult notions to grasp. In fact, they're beyond grasp, and that's indeed why they're so difficult to understand for our minds accustomed to concepts. If we can't manage to classify something in one or another category, we simply can't understand it. Since ultimate nature is beyond all categories and concepts, there's in a way "nothing" to understand! As long as we still hope to understand "something" that we can hold and put neatly in one of the drawers of our mind, we haven't understood the teachings yet. We need a lot of patience to develop a very broad mind, which will give us access to this level of understanding.

Fourth Paramita: Diligence

Tsöndru is usually translated as "diligence." In the Buddhist context, however, this term has a much wider connotation. It implies not only exerting effort and being industrious but also feeling interest and enthusiasm for positive actions. Diligence is finding joy in doing positive things.

Diligence is crucial. One can be generous, virtuous, disciplined, and even patient, but without diligence one won't succeed; one won't be of any great help to others. Diligence, interest, and joy in positive actions are like the motor of the other paramitas. When combined with diligence, they become effective and powerful.

Diligence is also the exact opposite of laziness. Being diligent means rejecting laziness.

There are three types of laziness:

1. The first is inactivity, inertia. We all have a list of things we put off until tomorrow. That which is called *lelo* in Tibetan denotes a strong tendency toward idleness, sleeping late, taking siestas, and indulging in little daily comforts, entertainment, and distractions. These idlers take great pleasure in everything negative or neutral. Too self-indulgent, they always manage not to do what they should. The antidote to this type of laziness is the awareness of impermanence, the temporary nature of things, the brevity of life, and the imminence of death, which can strike us at any moment. If we don't want to be assailed by anguish and regrets when confronted by death, we should progress in our spiritual development and begin to practice without delay. If we continually put things off until later, we run a big risk of being like the monk in the following story:

A Tibetan monk had as a friend a sort of spirit that we call *therang* in Tibetan. These dark and very hairy goblins have only one foot and love to play dice. It is said that, in order to make friends with one of them, one should go to a place where three rivers converge, throw dice, and repeat, "I win; the therang loses!" until the temptation gets too strong for the therang, who holds out his big hairy hand and says, "No! I'm not losing! Give me the dice!" One must then grab his hand and say, "I won't let you go unless you become my friend!" Thus a therang and this monk had become friends. They lived together in the monastery, the therang bringing the monk everything he wanted. The monk lived very happily in luxury. Although he knew very well that he should practice, he would postpone it all the time. He told his friend, "Certainly I am very happy right now, but I must practice to prepare for death. Warn me as soon as you see my death approaching." The therang agreed.

Months and years passed until one day the therang said to his friend, "Lama, do you realize your hair has gone gray?" The monk replied, "Of course my hair is gray. I'm getting old!" The therang went off, thinking, "Everything is OK, he knows." A few years later, the therang told him, "Lama, you're losing your teeth." The monk replied: "Of course I'm losing my teeth. I am getting old!" The therang thought: "If he knows this, all is well." One day, the therang announced to his friend that he was going to die on the following day. The monk got angry and reproached his friend: "Why didn't you tell me earlier? I asked you to warn me!" The therang replied, "But I warned you loads of times. First I told you your hair was going gray—you told me you were getting old, so I thought you realized. Then I told you your teeth were falling out, and again you told me you knew. I warned you many times!" This time the monk was seriously anxious, but what could he do now with so little time left?

This type of laziness is treacherous because illusions lull us into a sense of security. We truly believe we're going to do everything we should, but, for one reason or another, we're always putting things off until later. In order to avoid falling into this trap, we must stimulate our diligence.

Shantideva has this to say on the subject:

How quickly we react when a snake suddenly falls into our lap! Let's counter laziness and torpor with as much vivacity, before it penetrates [to our very core].

Let's practice diligently as soon as we can, knowing that the clock is ticking.

2. The second type of laziness is discouragement. This is when we think, "I'll never be able to become a bodhisattva, reach enlightenment, or free all beings from suffering. Why do I worry about all that when I'm unable to solve my own problems? I have my own problems; what can I do about all that goes wrong in the world?" Such thoughts make us lazy. The magnitude of the task paralyzes us. Everything seems too

difficult. In order to counter this type of laziness, let's remember there's not a single reason to be discouraged. In fact, all beings, down to the smallest of insects, have buddha nature. If we truly do our best, everything is possible, even reaching the noblest and the highest of all goals, enlightenment.

3. The third type of laziness is distraction. This is a matter of spending all our time at tasks that are of little or no importance. We give priority to the wrong objectives. We spend too much time on little things and not enough on what is essential. Keeping very busy, we run around like headless chickens doing nothing worthwhile.

Some lamas call the first type of laziness "Indian-style laziness" and this last type "Western-style laziness." In India, one lies in one's hammock under a large banyan and dozes, a little transistor at one's ear, waking up from time to time to call for one of those small clay cups of tea that one simply throws away when one is finished drinking. In the West one is constantly busy but most of the time without attending to what's really vital. One almost needs to make an appointment to see one's wife, one's husband, or one's children. One is very busy but not necessarily diligent. In order to avoid this type of laziness, one must sort out one's priorities and decide on whether an activity is really essential in order to solve one's problems or whether it is not a source of yet more suffering and boredom.

Gampopa subdivides diligence into three categories:

1. Diligence similar to an armor,
2. Diligence applied to activity, and
3. Insatiable diligence.

Diligence similar to an armor is the strength of our motivation. This is our statement of intention: "From now on, I'll never stop working or practicing until I've brought all sentient beings to complete liberation from all suffering. First I'll purify myself, then I'll practice the six paramitas and meditate, which will prepare me to help all other beings."

It is called an armor by analogy. In the past, thanks to their armors, warriors could enter into combat without being stopped or wounded.

In the same way, if we wear the armor of diligence, if our motivation is very strong, no obstacle, whatever it is, can stop us. With this first type of diligence, we are prepared to face the challenges that await us.

In a general way, we react according to our expectations. If we expect everything to be easy and pleasant, the smallest problem will discourage us. On the other hand, if we know that great difficulties and many important obstacles are ahead, we won't be discouraged by the first problem we encounter. The difficulties will seem small because we were expecting much worse! This applies to all situations in life. We usually expect too much from situations and people, with resulting problems! On the other hand, if we have no particular expectations, the smallest positive event will make us happy. A simple unexpected gentle word is then a source of joy because it pleasantly surprises us.

To put on the armor of diligence is a suitable way to prepare oneself. The least we can say is that, to become a bodhisattva, to try to help oneself and all sentient beings throughout space to reach the greatest happiness (that is, enlightenment) is not an easy task! It is a vast, noble, and grandiose objective. We must prepare ourselves to face all sorts of problems, big and small, without ever being discouraged, hence the necessity to don that armor of diligence.

The second type of diligence is applied diligence and this comes in three large fields.

1. Our first task is to apply ourselves to eliminating mental poisons. These negative emotions (hatred, attachment, pride, jealousy, greed, and so on) are our lifelong enemies, which, in life after life, have caused us and still cause us misery and suffering. All our efforts must be directed toward that target. How to proceed? Gampopa gives the following example: suppose you're walking and carrying a bowl filled to the brim with sesame seeds, followed by a man threatening to run you through with a sword if you lose as much as one seed. . . . In such a situation, wouldn't you walk with total concentration, taking great care not to let anything fall? We need the same degree of concentration and attention in order to fight our mental poisons, because they are the most powerful and dangerous enemies we have.

Gampopa lists the five qualities that should characterize our "strike." We must be stable and constant, devoid of pride, filled with devotion, and unshakable, and we must never turn back.

Stability and constancy in our approach help us to progress in our practice and not give it up. It means practicing in a regular manner, applying ourselves to it daily. Such perseverance enables us to remain insensitive to frustration and distraction.

We shouldn't consider our practice as something exceptional, think we are better than others and develop pride. We're simply doing what we should, what we decided would be the best thing to do for ourselves as well as for others, and we fulfill our commitment. There's no reason to feel proud of this. Let's beware of falling into the trap of this most vicious mental poison.

Devotion allows us to persevere with joy, enthusiasm, and interest.

We must equally remain unshakable. No difficulty, no suffering, no emotional turmoil should distract us from our target. We should simply carry on and never turn back. Whatever the obstacles or whoever the people trying to stop us, we shouldn't pay any attention. Even if everything around us seems to collapse, nothing should discourage us. While expecting obstacles, we should not feel disheartened when they appear.

2. The second sphere in which we should apply ourselves is that of the accumulation of merit.

3. The third sphere is that of applied diligence for the benefit of others. These two spheres are linked. If we apply ourselves with diligence to the benefit of others, we will inevitably accumulate merit. We should also encourage others to act in the same way, not only to work unremittingly but also to keep a positive attitude and to practice with joy.

The last type of diligence is an insatiable energy that brings the preceding two to completion. We mustn't be complacent with ourselves. We must go right to the end, realize the ultimate goal—total enlightenment—and bring all other beings to that state. On our way, we may experience blissful states, meet celestial beings, enter different types of samadhi, and progress through the different bhumis, but we must not stop at any of these experiences because none of them is the ultimate objective on which we are fixed. Our target is the highest of accomplishments: perfect enlightenment.

This insatiable diligence is a form of competition, but not in the usual sense. Usually, we compete with rivals in order to determine their level and try to be better than they are. If they're just average, we'll exert just enough effort to be a little better than they are, whereas in this case, we look neither left nor right. We compete with ourselves. We concentrate only on our objective and do all we can to reach it.

Diligence should also be purified in order to become a paramita. By purification we mean mixing everything we do—including diligently practicing—with the understanding of the true nature of everything. It means seeing our diligence as shunyata, emptiness, and being able to combine this understanding with the aspiration of compassion. Compassion and emptiness. Emptiness is the true nature. We should recognize shunyata as the true nature of everything, as interdependence, and at the same time be continuously inspired by compassion. Practiced in this way, diligence reaches its highest level and can be called the paramita of diligence.

Again, the effect of our diligence can be multiplied thanks to the skillful means of dedication. If we practice with a little diligence but with the right attitude and understanding and if we dedicate our practice with a pure mind, the result is thus multiplied and can become very great.

To practice with diligence allows us to quickly reach enlightenment. This is the ultimate result. The immediate, temporary, karmic result will be to allow us to achieve with success whatever we wish as long as we stay in samsara.

Fifth Paramita: Meditation

Even if we can master the four paramitas mentioned previously, without meditation our mind will stay out of control and under the influence of distraction. Distraction opens the door to all the disturbing emotions, and we're in danger of falling under the power of the mind poisons. It will then be impossible to get out of samsara, to free ourselves from confusion, and even to help others. Indeed, unless we develop a very strong and stable meditation, we won't develop clairvoyance, the capacity to read other people's minds—a very important capacity if we wish to help them.

All schools of Buddhism teach us to first develop the meditation of mental calm,[36] or *shamatha*, which makes our mind clear by calming the turmoil that permanently agitates it. Once we've achieved this stability, we can develop the meditation of profound vision,[37] *vipashyana*, which allows us finally to understand the true nature of things, shunyata. This understanding allows us to cut the root of the mental poisons, the disturbing emotions. Actually, all the different methods of meditation that we may encounter can all be categorized into either shamatha, vipashyana, or the combination of the two.

Of these two, vipashyana is closer to the sixth paramita, wisdom, because it consists of insight into the true nature of things. However, we cannot achieve it without first developing a strong, stable meditation of mental calm.

To experience the true nature of things and to have a simple intellectual understanding of it are two totally different things. We can have a conceptual idea of what the true nature of phenomena may be through intellectual understanding, but that may not have anything to do with a real experience of this true nature. We have to experience it, and this isn't possible without meditation, because a true understanding of the nature of things can take place only when the mind is perfectly stable and clear. When our mind is totally under our control, in a state of clarity and stability, we can turn our gaze inward and see its true nature. This experience is what we call the *prajnaparamita,* or paramita of wisdom, and also the ultimate bodhichitta. Therefore our preparation is crucial.

To achieve this stable shamatha meditation requires two conditions: the solitude of body and the solitude of mind.

Solitude of body, or physical isolation, implies placing ourselves at a distance from our normal activities, from the things we are attached to. We should find a place where we won't be distracted. In the context of daily city life, this means finding some corner or room where we'll be sheltered from distractions and disturbances and finding some time to meditate, setting aside all our daily busyness, our worries and mundane preoccupations. To be able to find that kind of time and space can be even more important in the context of a busy, active, mundane life than in the context of a contemplative life. Traditional Buddhist writings stipulate that we should go physically far away from everyday activities, places, things, and people to whom we are attached. To really meditate and to achieve results, we should ideally withdraw to a solitary place, defined by the text as "five hundred furlongs away from any towns or villages."

However, an isolated spot is not the only condition. If the mind is not peaceful, the place will make no difference. This is why the second condition is mental isolation. Even if the first condition of physical isolation is fulfilled, if we're constantly thinking of what we should do or say, of things we're attached to, of our expectations and fears, our minds are busy all the time and we can't possibly meditate correctly. Perhaps you've already heard of Drukpa Kunle, a celebrated "crazy" yogi. His brother, a very high and very traditional lama, wished him to make a retreat in order to reform his habits of living extravagantly and outside the norm. Drukpa Kunle accepted, and the two brothers began a strict retreat together, each meditating in his own separate room. One day, early in the morning, Drukpa Kunle left his cell and went down the road to Lhasa. The attendant came running to warn the lama, who sent someone straight away after Drukpa Kunle to bring him back. He immediately asked him for an explanation. Drukpa Kunle answered, "I went to look for you, thinking you were on the road to Lhasa, trying to dye yak tails red." Actually, while he was meditating in his cell, the lama had seen a yak tail nailed to the wall and thought, "The next time I go to Lhasa I'll dye it red and attach it to the head of my mule. That will be very attractive." In Tibet, it's a custom to decorate the heads of mules with yak tails dyed in red. Drukpa Kunle was a great *siddha*[38] able to read the thoughts of others; and knowing what was going on in his brother's mind, he had pretended to go to Lhasa to tease him and mock his distraction. Simply sitting in an isolated cell means nothing at all about the quality of our meditation.

There are many stories about crazy yogis. Drukpa Kunle lived beyond mundane conventions and behaved rather badly according to people's opinions. He did things that a monk is not supposed to do, but he was an enlightened being. It's very difficult to tell who's a crazy yogi and who's just a crazy man. The best criterion is perhaps to find out if this person is affected by the eight worldly dharmas. Is he worried about his public image and obsessed with fame, glory, and riches? Does he love praise and dislike indifference or criticism? If yes, he may be crazy, but he's certainly not a crazy yogi. On the other hand, if he has none of these traits, he may be crazy too, but there may be a little bit of "yoginess" in him.

The solitude of the mind is crucial for meditation. During our meditation sessions, even and especially if it's only for a very short moment, we must leave behind all our daily activities, get rid of our preoccupations, and not plan what we should do. If the mind jumps from one thing to another, our meditation will never be truly stable.

The first stage is to recognize which mental poison affects us the most. Is it possessiveness, hatred, ignorance? To counteract the dominant poison we should apply the appropriate antidote. The following three methods are the traditional techniques recommended by most Buddhist schools.

If possessiveness and attachment are our main problem, we should meditate on the ugly, least attractive aspects of what we're attached to. For example, if we're particularly attached to our body, we should analyze what it is made of and dissect it mentally. If we were to take off the skin, what would it look like? Would it still be attractive? The same technique can be used to lessen our attachment to someone else. Beauty is often what awakens desire and attachment in us, but when we take a closer look, what we think is very nice and beautiful may not actually be there. "Nice" and "beautiful" are just projections of our own mind. Beauty and the consequent attraction we feel don't really exist. When we consider a person or a thing to be very nice, beautiful, or attractive, we tend to think of it more and more. Consequently, it becomes more and more important in our eyes, and we can even become attached to the point that we think we can no longer live without it. When we look closer, more rationally, at the object of such an attachment, we can see its true nature, and we'll discover that it's in fact neither as beautiful nor as different nor as important as we initially thought. Everything's a question of point of view, and if we consider from another angle, we could even end up thinking it is actually ugly and repulsive.

People who are dominated by hatred and anger should meditate on loving-kindness and compassion according to the techniques I explained earlier.

People who are dominated by jealousy should meditate on equanimity, the tranquillity of the mind, and rejoice in the luck and good fortune of others.

Those inclined to vanity or pride should exchange their qualities, their goods, and their advantages for the flaws of others.

Finally, if ignorance is predominant, we should meditate on the twelve links of interdependent origination.[39] If everything seems very solid and existing in an independent way, or if we're too selfish, we should contemplate and analyze these twelve links. We'll then understand that there's nothing that's not interdependent, interrelated, and we'll learn to see things as they really are, devoid of self-existence. Nothing exists in itself; everything is shunyata. What we mean by shunyata and by dependent origination or conditioned production are the same.

Let's consider an object, any object, a watch, for example. What is it made of? Where is the watch? If we take it apart, will it still exist as a watch? This is the hand, but it's not the watch. This is the glass, but it's not the watch. None of the elements of this watch are in themselves the watch. It's an assembly of different pieces, but no one piece is the watch. We could use the same reasoning for each piece of the watch. For example, if I take the glass of the watch and crush it into its different elements, there's no more glass, only the components of glass. If the glass is reduced to dust, we have dust, but no glass. And even this powder, if we take the tiniest grain of dust, isn't independently existing either, because we can still grind it and reduce it into finer particles. We could think that, having arrived at the level of the atom, we could find a basic material particle, because if there is nothing solid to start with, how can anything come into existence? The classic question, which we find in the tradition, is whether the smallest possible particle has sides or not. In fact, in order to be conceived as such, the smallest possible particle must still occupy volume in space and have sides, angles, and so on. If a particle exists materially, it necessarily has a shape, a mass, an upper and a lower side, and so on, and as long as it shows different sides, there must be a way to decompose it. We can continue to fragment the atom until nothing solid or material exists. But without mass or form, we can't have matter. How can particles without mass or form constitute a substance? It's necessary that a particle has elements to combine with others and form something, but once it has such components, this particle can be decomposed. Its existence is therefore interdependent. To come back to the watch, it's not "really" there if we analyze it as we have just done; there's no one independent thing that can be pointed out as "the watch." There is no core, no essence to it. It's only composed of a series of elements and doesn't exist on its own. "Watch" is a label we use to name a group of interdependent elements.

Everything is interdependent. Many things coming together give us the impression that there is one object. Nevertheless there's nothing, not even the smallest thing, that can be isolated and shown to exist in an independent manner. We see things, we touch them, we "feel" them, as long as they are "there," but if we analyze them, we find nothing, no indestructible particle, that could exist in an independent way. All is shunyata, emptiness, because nothing has any substance.

The same goes for our mind. To say that the nature of this watch is emptiness doesn't mean that this watch does not exist at all, but that each element of which it is made is composed of many others, and that its existence is by nature interdependent. This is why the philosophy of interdependence and emptiness are one and the same thing, simply approached from two different angles. If you understand the philosophy of interdependence, then you see the true nature of things. The twelve links of conditioned production analyze interdependence from a personal point of view. This would take too long to discuss here, but I invite you to read more on this subject.

In a simple and general way, if our meditation is disturbed by thoughts (either negative or positive), we should try to calm our mind through the meditation of mental calm, which comprises different methods of relaxation and concentration, like breathing exercises.

There are many ways of dealing with negative emotions. Those that have been transmitted by the oral tradition of Marpa and Milarepa as the six yogas of Naropa have a particular importance.

All methods of meditation have the same objective, whether they belong to Theravada, Mahayana, or Vajrayana: to calm and stabilize the mind and control negative emotions. It's for this reason that I believe everyone can practice more than one tradition simultaneously.

There's a well-known story on this subject. When the great Indian scholar Atisha arrived in Tibet, he asked his new students what they'd already studied. They gave him an impressive list of texts, treatises, tantras, and so on. Atisha was pleased and a little surprised. "You've already studied so much that my presence here is totally useless. You've already received all the teachings!" Then he asked, "How do you practice what you have learned?" They answered, "We always practice according to what is said in each teaching, in each tantra, sutra, or text." Atisha then understood the usefulness of his presence in Tibet.

The thing is, if one doesn't know how to integrate the different practices into one, then all these teachings become a source of confusion. We shouldn't see them as separate elements but as supporting one another, like different facets of one and the same practice. It's only then that a profusion of different practices won't create confusion. Actually, what we call practice is nothing other than working on our emotions;

it's our effort to find a solution to our own problems. There is no other practice. Whether we call it Tara, Amitabha, *zazen*, vipashyana, or something else doesn't make any difference. What really makes the difference is how the practice affects our minds and whether it helps us solve our emotional problems. The practice that really helps us could be vipashyana or Tara or Mahamudra. The spiritual guide is not there to impose his practice, his path; he's there to guide us on our own. There are as many paths as there are practitioners. We can try to attack our mental poisons from many different angles at a time and see which gives the best results. This doesn't mean, however, that we should mix everything up. A practitioner of Mahamudra should keep this practice as a foundation, but this shouldn't stop him or her from using other methods if necessary, from finding inspiration elsewhere in order to deepen, increase, and enrich his or her main practice. This inspiration need not have anything to do with Buddhism; it could be something completely different, like science, art, physical exercise, gardening, or anything else.

This doesn't mean mixing the techniques but concentrating on those we've chosen and giving them all the depth and force possible. The problems are ours, and the solution is therefore ours as well. If you need to open a can of food and you don't have a can opener, you will try to open it with a knife. If you still can't manage, you'll try to open it with scissors. If this still doesn't work, you'll try something else. The most important thing is to open the can. It's possible you'll need all those utensils, but you might need just one. However, if we don't understand how to do it, if we're not able to realize this unity in our practice, it's then preferable to limit ourselves to one practice.

We can distinguish three stages[40] of meditation:

The first stage is called remaining happily in the present. Meditation means relaxing, letting go—but without distraction! Our mind may need a support to fix its attention, such as breathing, the mind itself, or any kind of object, either external or visualized. If a particular support suits us, it's sufficient to let our mind gently settle on it. If we don't need such a support, we can simply "be," on our own, completely relaxed. When the relaxation is total, there can be no distraction or concentration. When there's distraction and/or concentration, the relaxation is not complete. Meditation is defined as total relaxation without distraction or dullness.

Basically, meditation has two enemies: distraction and dullness. Have you ever seen the excellent picture that illustrates the stages of meditation? We see an elephant, a rabbit, a monkey, and a man. The elephant is our mind, the rabbit is dullness, the monkey is distraction, and the man is attention. At the bottom of the page the monkey is pulling the elephant by a rope wherever he wants. The man tries in vain to catch him, running far behind the elephant. Even if he's conscious of the situation, for the moment he can do nothing. Nevertheless, from picture to picture, he manages to catch up slowly and put a rope around the elephant's neck. The monkey and then the rabbit are slowly left behind. And at one point, the man climbs on the elephant's back; he's in charge, he rides the elephant and charges down with the blazing sword of wisdom to liberate all the beings of samsara. He gets complete control. Through meditation we succeed in subduing and training our body and our mind. When we've perfectly mastered the body and the mind, the strength of the mind is such that we can do what we wish. Through its power, we're capable of controlling our environment both mentally and physically. If we wish, we can even accomplish what are considered miracles. This is the first stage of meditation: we're completely in control of all that surrounds us and feel perfectly happy in the present moment.

This first stage is divided into four levels, or *dhyana*. Without going into detail, we can say that the first level is characterized by the presence of analytical and discursive thoughts. The second level is characterized by an experience of joy and delight. At the third level, an impression of contentment or satisfaction replaces the joy and the happiness. At the fourth level, even this consciousness disappears, leaving nothing in its place but a great peace, a great serenity and equanimity.

The second stage is called acquiring qualities. It comprises different qualities and the different powers achieved through meditation.

The third stage is working for the benefit of others. At this stage, we develop, thanks to meditation, the powers that will help us benefit others. When we speak of the emanations of buddhas and bodhisattvas and the miracles they accomplish, we should understand that we're talking about the results of meditation, of the manifestation of the power of a perfectly mastered mind.

The dedication is as important for meditation as it is for the other paramitas. We should always dedicate all our meditation sessions to the happiness of all sentient beings and make the wish that one day we'll be capable of guiding them all out of samsara. The length of our sessions counts less than the degree of calm we have achieved and the good motivation we develop through dedication.

Sixth Paramita: Wisdom[41]

Wisdom, or discriminative awareness, is the sixth paramita. Gampopa presents it in seven sections:

1. The faults or shortcomings of having no wisdom and the qualities and benefits of understanding it,
2. A description of the essential characteristics of wisdom,
3. The different aspects of wisdom,
4. The essential characteristics of each of these aspects,
5. What has to be known, how to get a deep understanding or realization of that wisdom,
6. How to assimilate that understanding, how to become one with it, and
7. The consequences or results of having understood and integrated wisdom.

Benefits and Disadvantages   The first section discusses the benefits and disadvantages of having some or no understanding of wisdom.

The prajnaparamita is seeing the truth as it is, seeing things as they really are. If it's absent, nothing can help us, which is why it's so important to develop it. All the other paramitas don't become paramitas, don't become transcendent, if we don't have at least a slight realization of what *prajna* means. Prajna, or wisdom, is described as the main medium through which we can liberate ourselves from the samsaric state. Without wisdom, we can't free ourselves from the sufferings caused by our wrong way of reacting. Our main problem is ignorance, confusion. If we can't get rid of ignorance, there's no chance that we'll get any form of release.

This is why wisdom is compared to an eye. With eyes, you see things and can lead others on the right path. If you're blind, no matter how many good qualities you have and even if your other sense faculties are intact, you're unable to see where you're going.

Gampopa quotes many texts to illustrate this point. For instance, *The Abridged Prajnaparamita*[42] says: "How could even a trillion blind persons ever reach the city without a guide and not knowing the way? Without wisdom to show them the way, the five eyeless paramitas are without a guide and unable to lead to enlightenment."

All the other paramitas, what we call the methods or the right means, remain incomplete without the wisdom: they don't work; they don't lead to the right destination. Nevertheless, if we only concentrate on the wisdom aspect without developing generosity, adopting the right conduct, and so on, wisdom alone won't lead us to liberation either. Mahayana Buddhism strongly emphasizes the union of both means and wisdom. The means, or methods, are compared to the feet of a person, whereas the wisdom is compared to the eyes. If we wish to go somewhere, we need both feet and eyes. Even with good eyes, we'll be unable to start our journey if we can't walk. With good feet but without eyes, we may start walking, but we won't know where our steps lead us and we may fall at any time. We need both. The methods and the wisdom are equally important. If one is missing, the other becomes incomplete; this is the main message.

Gampopa also quotes the *Sutra Requested by Akshayamati*:[43]

With wisdom lacking means, one is tied to nirvana.
With means lacking wisdom, one is tied to samsara.
Therefore the combination of both is needed.

In Mahayana, we often talk about the ultimate truth and the relative truth. It's sometimes misunderstood.

When we talk about the ultimate or absolute truth, it means that when we analyze, when we look deeply into things, we see that there's no substance, nothing really existing. We can't find the "reality" of things. This is what the prajnaparamita tells us. However, if we get only a superficial, intellectual understanding of this notion, we may sometimes develop the idea that nothing exists at all and that we therefore don't need to do anything. If we get trapped in such a mode of thought (which is traditionally called the nihilistic view), we won't develop our potential fully in a wholesome way. We'll consider it unnecessary to work on ourselves and to accumulate positive deeds and karma. We won't make any effort to improve, which will prevent our progress.

On the other hand, if we concentrate only on positive deeds, if we're very anxious to help others but do so without any understanding of the real nature of things, of impermanence and selflessness, we'll get too involved with the worldly, mundane aspect of things and we won't be able to keep whatever we're doing in perspective. That's the main problem. We may be doing something very good, very beneficial, such as social work, but we can become so involved with it that it becomes a great problem for us. We can get so attached to what we're doing that it becomes a bondage. Therefore, if we wish to become completely free, developed, and awakened beings, we have to develop both sides.

In order to generate the understanding of the prajnaparamita, we should apply what we traditionally call the three ways:

1. Listening to and studying texts and teachings,
2. Contemplating and reflecting on those teachings, and
3. Meditating to integrate the understanding gained through the previous two.

But applying these alone won't allow us to develop the realization: we must simultaneously develop the means—that is, accumulate positive deeds through the five other paramitas. Every positive thing we do will help us see the true nature of reality. Wisdom is not something that we can gain only through listening, reflecting, and meditating.

Essential Characteristics   We now come to the second point: the essential characteristics of prajna. Prajna means more than wisdom. It has sometimes been translated as "discriminative awareness," which is a good translation because to discriminate means to be aware of what is true and what is not. However, "wisdom" is the translation that has been adopted most widely, and people usually understand what it means. "Discriminative awareness" may be closer to the literal meaning, however.

Jna in Sanskrit means "knowledge." *Pra* means "very," "much," "the best." Prajna is the highest, the best, the supreme knowledge. The Tibetan word, *sherab*, is a literal translation of the Sanskrit.

The main characteristic of prajna is an accurate discernment or appreciation of phenomena, which means that one sees clearly and vividly the true nature of things.

Different Aspects   Wisdom has three distinct aspects, what Gampopa calls:

1. The worldly wisdom,
2. The lesser supramundane wisdom, and
3. The higher supramundane wisdom.

Characteristics of Each Aspect   Let's look at the essential characteristics of each of these aspects of wisdom.

1. Wisdom has a worldly aspect that corresponds to the best of the relative human knowledge. A vast, clear knowledge of logic, medicine, science, and linguistics belongs to the field of prajna. In India and Tibet,

knowledge was traditionally divided into four branches or domains: the sciences of healing, logic, linguistics, and creative skills. However, when we talk about wisdom in the context of Dharma, we have more in mind than these relative facets of human knowledge. There are more absolute aspects, and worldly wisdom is considered a first step.

2. What Gampopa calls the lesser supramundane wisdom includes what we understand through study, reflection, and meditation, for instance, the realization of impermanence and the interdependence of all phenomena, the understanding that there is no lasting peace and happiness within samsara.

The realization of selflessness, of the nonexistence of ego, is also part of this second aspect of wisdom. We all have this feeling of existing as distinct, separate entities. This is what makes us say, "I am." However, if we look carefully at ourselves, we'll discover that we're also made of many constituents and that there's nothing inside our body or mind that we can pinpoint and identify as "I." Is there anything in whatever we see, whatever we can think of, any material or immaterial thing that is completely *one*, permanent and independent? Can we find just one thing that has those characteristics? If we can't, it means that nothing is permanent, that everything changes all the time. It means that everything is compounded, made of many parts. We may think that this book is one, but it is made of many pages. Each page is itself made of different substances, covered with symbols printed with ink. Ink and paper are again combinations of different substances. Everything can be taken apart until almost nothing remains. This means that nothing is independent. Everything exists through the help of many other things. If only one element is missing, the whole changes or disappears. All phenomena, including ourselves, are interdependent.

This is the true nature of things: they clearly appear without having any substantial existence. This is not something we create, or some Buddhist theory or dogma that we try to impose—it's the way things really are. When things that are not one are taken to be one, when what's dependent is taken as independent, when what is impermanent is taken as permanent, this is what we call ignorance or confusion. We are conditioned to see things in this ignorant, confused way, and we react according to this conditioning by feeling either desire or aversion, by constantly running after or away from things. It is most important to get rid of this wrong view, so as to free ourselves from these habitual patterns.

3. The third aspect of wisdom is the higher or great supramundane wisdom, the full understanding of the unborn nature of things. We should assiduously tend to gain that ultimate understanding.

How to Realize Wisdom In order to gain this higher form of wisdom, we should first abandon our belief in substantial reality.

A clearer understanding of the true nature of things, even if very limited, can already benefit us greatly. We may not yet have any experiential understanding of the way things really are, but we may have already become a little suspicious about the way things appear to us. We can have a doubt as to their permanence, as to the way they seem to be separate entities. This will somewhat loosen our strong attachment to things and we'll become less tense, less anxious.

Let's think, for example, of the way memories of the past affect us. If we believe that what we've been in the past, what we are now, and what we'll be tomorrow are one and the same entity, if we posit the identity of the "I" throughout past, present, and future, then whatever has affected us in the past still affects us now and will go on affecting us in the future. Maybe we think our parents treated us badly when we were children and we still resent their abuse today, although nobody would recognize us looking at a picture of the child we were then. We always tend to think that we're the same as we were thirty years ago, as yesterday and tomorrow. Even when we die, we still think we're the same person. Because of this identification, what happened in our youth may still affect us. Of course, what I am now is also caused by what I was yesterday, but I'm not exactly the same as I was yesterday. If I understand more clearly that I'm changing all the time, then whatever happened in my past won't affect me now. If I had to undergo lots of trouble and pain, all right, it's gone now. True, I'm what I am because of that past; I'm "caused" by my past—this is what we call karma, and karma is not something written on my forehead. I am my karma; I'm the result of all that happened to me before; but still, I'm not that past. What was yesterday was yesterday. What is today is today. Today's river is not yesterday's river, and none of the water that flowed by yesterday is still here today. Everything changes from one second to the next, but if we identify with our past, then we're still affected by everything that happened to us and we carry the huge burden of our whole past. When we understand that we're no longer the child who suffered so much, we can put down our burden and be free.

We're all confronted with choices and decisions in our daily life, and we all wish to make the right choice, to have the wisest reaction. Here too the understanding of selflessness can help us to deal with concrete situations. When we say that the "I" doesn't exist, it doesn't mean that we don't exist at all but that we don't exist in the way we think we do. It doesn't mean that there's nothing: you can see me; I can see you. If we really understand deeply that what we call the "I" isn't just one permanent identity but many different things that are changing all the time, then as a by-product, we'll be less self-centered, less selfish, and less tense. In order to apply our understanding to concrete situations, we first have to integrate this understanding. Our way of seeing things changes little by little. It comes naturally. If somebody says something unpleasant to me, why should I get angry? Suppose someone shouts at me, "You're a dog!" and I get angry thinking, "How dare he say I'm a dog? I'm not!" But why should I get so upset? His insult won't turn me into a dog! I won't start barking and growing hair all over! Anger comes from my strong conviction that "I" shouldn't be insulted, that "I" should be praised and respected. When we understand this more and more, we'll no longer care so much and get angry so easily, even when we're insulted. Of course, if you listen to only a few teachings, your understanding will remain superficial, and when you actually get angry, simply thinking, "I'm not there, my opponent's not there" won't work at all. You have to deepen your understanding now, when you're not under the control of strong emotions. You have to learn, reflect, practice, and train so that you don't get angry when provoked in the first place. The habit developed through practice will make you aware of the situation and allow you to check your instinctive reaction. Regular practice will lessen your pride and self-centeredness. Being less proud, you won't be so easily hurt, and you won't flare up in anger at the first unpleasant word.

We also often think of ourselves as a son, a father, a mother, a lawyer, a teacher, and so on. We usually identify with a certain role, but are we limited to this role? We can be many different things at the same time. When we say, "This is me," is this "me" existing separately, apart from these different roles, or is it just one and the same thing?

Our habit of considering ourselves as an identity, of identifying with a name, is deeply anchored. Let's take "Peter," for instance. He talks, feels, and thinks. To say that Peter has no "self-entity" doesn't mean that Peter doesn't exist at all. My goal is not to negate his existence but to try to find out who Peter really is, to see what the real nature of his existence is. When we say, "This is Peter," is there some real "Peter essence" anywhere, or is it a particular voice, a certain face, style, and hairdo, many things put together that we label as "Peter"? Peter could be called John, Paul, Ringu Tulku, or anything. For different reasons, we started to call that particular person "Peter"; we think he's Peter, and he thinks of himself as Peter. And whatever comes from him is "Peter's." Now, what Peter has to do if he really wants to come to know his own nature is to look at himself. This doesn't mean that once Peter knows his true nature, he'll cease to exist as Peter. He'll continue to be Peter for all of us and for himself, but his way of seeing his identity will have shifted a little: he'll see thoughts as thoughts, feelings as feelings, and no longer mix things up in confusion. He'll see everything as it is, without binding things to concepts, without putting them into unnecessary structures and categories. His life will no longer be a constant struggle. He'll feel free. That's what we're talking about.

We examine who we really are while sitting in meditation. We analyze whether the different aspects we're made of are our ego or not. We consider a finger, for instance. Is this finger "me" or not? If this finger is "me," where can I locate this "I"? In the nail? The skin? The bone? Blood? Cells? Considered from that angle, we discover that there's no "I" and no finger. But if "I" am not the finger, can we find the "I" elsewhere in the body? If we can't, where is it? Most people will of course answer that it has to be searched for in the brain. But the brain is made of many cells. Which one can we identify as "I"? We thus come to the conclusion that there's no "I." What we call "I" is the interdependent play of many elements. When something arises in this way, we can say that at a relative level, "This is this," but if we look more deeply into it, we realize that it has no strong, real existence.

This intellectual understanding may help us lessen our attachments and fears, but as long as we haven't integrated this knowledge into our own experience, we won't get the full benefit of seeing selflessness. We may think, "Things are compounded and impermanent; things are infinite; things have no substantial existence," but we might just as well think the opposite. Whatever we think is just a construction of our mind. They're our own concepts. If we decide that the whole universe is empty of any self-entity, this is only our mind's projection. To say that everything is there, solid and existing, is nothing but another projection. When we say that we can see the endless universe, we may really believe that we're looking at the whole infinite universe, but we're actually just looking at an image we've made up in our imagination. All our assessments of things being one way or another are nothing but concepts. This is why the most important thing is our mind. It doesn't matter whether the things out there are real or not. Even "real" and "unreal" are concepts. When we say that something is real, what do we actually mean by this? It's just our own way of describing things. Whether we say that it's all real or it's all unreal, it comes to the same thing. The authority, the dictator, is our own mind. If we can understand and experientially "see" the true nature of our mind, we also see the true nature of everything else, because it's within our mind that we perceive everything.

As soon as we have a thought, an idea, or a feeling, we think, "This is my idea, my thought, my feeling," and the most important element becomes "me." If we can find the nature of this "me," we find out the nature of the mind. If we look deeply into a thought, any thought, is the thought "me," or is it different from me? Is there any mind besides the thought? A thought comes up, or a feeling or an emotion, and we immediately grasp it: "This is my thought, my feeling, my emotion," but do "I" exist separately from them? When the thought or the emotion dissolves, where is the "I"? Does it disappear with the mental event? And if it doesn't, where is it? These are most crucial questions!

Of course, there's no point in my stating, "There is nothing besides the mental events that come up," and you repeating after me, "Oh, yes, there's nothing beside it. The lama said there's nothing, so it's not there." This wouldn't work. Each of you has to conduct an investigation into the very heart of your own experience. What I tell you may be 100 percent correct or totally wrong—it doesn't matter. What matters is not what I tell you but what you yourself can discover through your own experience. Whatever you find out in this way, even if it's very little, will make a real difference. This is the main message. Look at what happens inside yourself!

A thought comes up, or a sensation. What happens? "Seeing" happens, then we apply a label: "I see this." We immediately infer a "seer," which is no other than the "I." Whatever arises is just a sensation, but besides that, we create a separate entity that we call "I." If we search for it, we may not find it anywhere, either inside or outside the body, or besides the feeling, the thought, or the emotion. Nevertheless, we deduce that because there's a thought there must be a thinker; because there's an experience there must be an experiencer: our ego. Actually, the experience itself is the experiencer. The experience itself is the action, the manifestation, but as soon as we've created the "experiencer," the action becomes a reaction. We say "I" am experiencing "this" and thus create an identity beside the experience itself. When we say, "This is a glass," we superimpose the label "glass" on the different parts that constitute it. We then add "a beautiful glass" or even a "very beautiful glass." We can create many different things on top of this glass. In the same way, we superimpose this separate identity on the continuous arising of all manifestations. Through various circumstances, different causes and effects, thoughts, feelings, and perceptions arise, on which we superimpose an ego that becomes the central, focal point. Because "I" am, then "they" are. This "I" is what I have to protect, and "they" have to be pushed away. If there's something I like among "them," I have to get it. If there's something I dislike, I reject it. This duality is what gives rise to hatred, fear, aversion, desire, craving, and the entire scope of our emotions, that is, to the whole samsaric mind we discussed earlier.

All this confusion, all the conflicts and sufferings inherent to the samsaric state of mind are based on the mistaken perception of an ego, a self, that we posit on top of manifestations. This identification of a self is what we call the basic ignorance, or sometimes the coemergent, "born-together" ignorance. It's the real initial source of our confusion. If it weren't there, no subsequent confusion could take place. The identification of a self, of a separate individuality, is the cause of the dualistic view that generates attachment and aversion. Gampopa defines that individuality as follows: "In fact what is referred to as a person is actually an unbroken continuum of self-reproducing aggregates accompanied by intelligence, a mischievous and cunning thing, always thinking and scheming, moving and scattering about." He also quotes the *Exhaustive Commentary of Authentic Knowledge*.[44] "The term *individual* applied to a continuum is in fact constant movement and scattering. When *I* exists, *other* will be known. Through the *I* and *other* pair comes clinging and aversion. Through the complex interaction of these will arise all harm."

When we posit this "I am" on top of or beside whatever arises, it's also a concept. It also comes from our knowledge, our confusion, information, memories of the past and projections over the future all mixed up. All these things make us assert, "I am like this" or "I am like that." That fixed individuality is only a concept, and it doesn't overlap with our actual experience. We should look at this very moment, at what we are right now, at what the true nature of our mind is. That's very difficult because we're not used to it, but it's actually the main meditation: to be able to see what we are in the present, in this very moment.

If we can look completely and directly at this very moment, not outside but inside, without going into the past or the future, leaving behind all the patterns of information, education, and culture that we carry with us from the past, it's said that we'll be able to see the true nature of what we are in a very uncomplicated, unconceptual way. As long as we bring in concepts, we mix things up. We may think and feel that we're seeing the whole truth, but we're actually just making it up in our mind.

To see the true enlightened nature of our mind isn't impossible and could even be very easy. It's just a matter of looking into our mind, experiencing it as it is right now, and that's it! But there are four reasons we don't see it.

The first reason is that it is too easy. We think that it's very difficult and complicated, something we have to struggle for. We think we have to do three, four, or even twelve years of retreat in a cave and go to the Himalayas in order to get it. Actually it's just here and now. It's too easy, and therefore we can't see it.

The second reason is that it's too near. When we think of enlightenment, it seems far away, many lifetimes ahead. Actually it's just here, in our consciousness at this very moment. We usually can't see what's too close to our eyes, like our eyebrows, for instance.

The third reason is that it's too good. It's completely free, without any problems, but we are so used to living in conflicts and problems that we finally got attached to them. They've become very important for us, and the struggle gives us a feeling of being truly alive. More or less consciously, we can't conceive of a life without problems.

The fourth reason is that it's too deep. We can't see things in their total dimension; we're used to seeing only small, scattered pieces, which we all put in the wrong place! We're not used to seeing the whole picture in a global perspective.

Seeing the truth will affect our way of reacting. As we explained before, we suffer because of a wrong way of reacting, one that originates from not seeing things as they are.

We talk about "Brussels," but, actually, where's the city if we take out the houses one by one? We decide to call "Brussels" all these houses put together, and it then becomes Brussels for you and me and everybody, in the same way that we decide to call a "forest" many trees put together. When we create one thing out of many, we make it very real and tend to react too strongly toward it. When we think of ourselves as "I," when we think, "This is me," we actually make ourselves the center of the world. The next moment, we assert, "This is my book, this is my throne, these are my students, this is my city, my world, my universe, I'm the greatest!" That's how we react all the time, isn't it? And we want to make "ours" whatever we like and to fight whatever we dislike. That's the problem.

If we're able to pull ourselves out of that way of reacting, if we're able to get a little less solid view of ourselves, we'll become less rigid and be able to deal with situations in a more flexible way. Our aim is to see things as they really are, not to negate their existence. To say that things don't exist, that there's nothing—no houses, no city, no men, no women—is not the point. It's wrong. If this was our aim, we'd better stop our spiritual practice at once. I may say that I'm "not truly existing," but what about my "being not there" when I'm getting hungry or thirsty or when my knees hurt during my meditation session? The point of this analysis is to understand what is happening when we say, "I am" or "I see this" or "I think like this." How is it happening? *How* is the important point. We come to realize that there's no "I" behind everything, doing, controlling, and masterminding it all, but that our sense of a separate individual existence comes from an amalgamation of many different things and situations, many causes and effects that come together in a flow. It has the same nature as a rainbow. When a rainbow appears, it's there; nobody can deny it. We can see it. However, the nature of the rainbow is such that nobody can touch it. A rainbow appears whenever the necessary conditions are gathered, but even while it can be seen in the sky, it's insubstantial; it has no real, solid existence. In the same way, everything we can see, experience, or think about is, in a way, like a rainbow. When all the necessary ingredients, the interdependent relative causes, are present, things appear. It's like chemistry: a certain reaction happens only when all the right ingredients and conditions are put together. If one of them is missing, nothing happens. Even while phenomena appear, they're constantly changing and ready to disappear. Anything can vanish at any time. Only one missing element can cause something to vanish. That's the nature of everything, of all phenomena, ourselves included. It's impossible to get hold of anything, to cling to it, to fasten and secure it.

If we understand this a little more deeply, a little more clearly, we'll become less grossly attached to things. We'll relax a little, and our way of reacting will change progressively. Confronted with something very frightening, we'll panic less because we'll know that what's coming is more like a shadow than something real. We'll also know that this "I" of ours isn't so real either. Why should something unreal be afraid of a shadow? It's all like a dream. In a nightmare, we may be terrified by a monster coming to tear us apart, but if we realize that it's only a dream, everything changes. We feel relieved, and even if the monster eats us up, it doesn't matter because we know we're all right—he can't really kill us. If in our ordinary life we come to understand, even in a superficial way, that things aren't as solid and real as they seem, our reactions change and we're no longer so strongly affected by what is bad and fearful or good and attractive. Both attachment and aversion decrease, whereas our freedom increases. We no longer get very excited when a little thing turns right, or very depressed when a little thing goes wrong. We get a greater calm and stability and we're better able to deal with the world.

We now understand that things have no real existence, that they're like a magic show or a dream, but it's still an intellectual understanding, a mind game. Having lessened our belief in the substantial reality of phenomena, we should beware of the belief in their unreality. To say that nothing exists is as wrong a view as saying that everything has a solid existence. Gampopa illustrates this with a quotation from Saraha: "To believe in reality is to be (stupid) like cattle, but to believe in unreality is even more stupid!"

The right view, the right understanding is to follow what is called the Middle Way, or Madhyamika in Sanskrit, which is not easy.

What we call "I" and "you," all actions, reactions, causes and effects, karma, everything, are all there. It's all happening, but it has an unreal quality—precisely because it's happening. This is logical in a way: if everything had a solid, substantial reality, there would be no scope for changes, everything would remain as it is. Precisely because things have no fixed reality, they can change and evolve all the time. This is why chemicals react: you put two different substances together and they react to produce a third substance thanks to their lack of self-existence. All this creativity, everything affecting everything else, all phenomena, can happen because there's no real existence. A small seed put in the ground grows into a huge tree that produces flowers and fruit. How could this happen if the seed was only a seed and nothing else? How can the seed become a plant? When the seed's still there, there's no plant, and when the plant is visible, the seed's no longer there. However, without the seed, the plant couldn't have grown. If the seed was just a seed, it couldn't give rise to a plant either; however, a seed isn't just one thing, and when it reacts with other conditions, the plant grows. It can be very big or very small, and it can give rise to many other things.

This explains why, from a Buddhist point of view, even time and space are relative and have no fixed, solid existence. Different events can simultaneously take place in the same space. This is illustrated by the story of Milarepa and the yak horn. Milarepa had a student called Rechungpa. Although Tibet is a very cold country, Milarepa had mastered the yogic technique of inner heat and he was wearing just one piece of cotton cloth even in the high mountains of the Himalayas. His student could do the same but he was smaller than Milarepa, which is why he was called Rechungpa. *Re* means "cotton" in Tibetan, and *chung* means "small." He was the "Small Cotton-Clad One." Milarepa had sent him to India to bring back teachings he hadn't received yet. Rechungpa came back with those teachings, but he had also brought back some books of black magic. Milarepa, who had come to welcome him on his way back, knew this and wanted to destroy those books that would only harm Rechungpa. He burned them while Rechungpa was fetching water, and when the latter learned this, he got very angry and resented Milarepa for having done so. On the ensuing trip back, he was walking behind his teacher, sulking. They had to cross a big plateau where nothing grew and there was no shelter. A yak horn lay on the ground, and Milarepa told Rechungpa to take it, that it might be useful soon. Rechungpa did so, grudgingly, thinking that his teacher had gone crazy, destroying valuable things and collecting worthless ones. When they reached the center of the plateau, a violent hailstorm broke out. Milarepa asked Rechungpa to put the horn on the ground and he quickly went into the horn for shelter. The horn didn't grow big and Milarepa didn't shrink. He just sat comfortably inside the horn, singing a song inviting Rechungpa to join him inside. How could this happen? How can one sit inside a yak horn without the horn growing any bigger or one becoming any smaller? Such seemingly impossible things can happen when one has the full understanding of the true nature of things.

The Middle Way means seeing things in a nonconceptual way. If I say that things really exist, that is a concept produced by my mind. If I say that nothing exists, that everything's unreal, that's also just a concept, an intellectual assessment. The real understanding of the truth is to see things directly as they really are. "Real" and "unreal" are only relative terms. When one says, "This is not real," it means that one automatically posits the existence of something that is "real" and then subsequently negates it. For instance, if you say, "There's no ghost in this house," you first assume that there's something called ghost, which actually exists, the presence of which you then negate. This reflects a dualistic approach and a superficial understanding. The assumption itself is wrong. It's only an intellectual and wrong view. Really seeing the truth can't be attained in this way. Through the intellect, one can approach the truth; one can presume that the truth must be something like this or like that, but one can't experience it. One has to come to it in an experiential way: that's the Middle Way.

The Middle Way isn't something "in between." It's called the Middle Way because it doesn't fall into any extreme view, any concept, solution, or idea. When we think of something, that idea seems very real. If I say "Calcutta," an image of Calcutta comes to your mind, but is it Calcutta? It would be far from it! Nevertheless, we usually mix up the image in our mind with reality. It's the same with everything we think of, like "This is good" or "This is bad." All these ideas are just mental images.

If we really want to see the truth, this can only be done without concepts. As soon as concepts creep in, things become images in our mind. This is why we talk about a nonconceptual way of seeing things and why it's so important.

This is also why philosophies never come to any convincing conclusion. They ask how the world came about, whether it comes from something or nothing. If they assert that it came from "something," where does that something come from? And if they state that it came from nothing, how can "something" come from "nothing"? This has been the main puzzle of all philosophies through the ages. As long as we don't look at the world as it is, as long as we don't find out what exactly it is, we'll never find an answer. Did the chicken come first, or the egg? There's no end to this—it can go on and on forever. These problems arise because of our initial assumption that the world is actually truly existing and that it must therefore originate from something. Once we have seen the true nature of things, such questions are not "solved," they simply dissolve.

The closest definition we can give of this true nature is "interdependence." "Interdependence" means the same as shunyata, or emptiness. In Buddhism, we always talk about emptiness, and usually people misinterpret it. Emptiness doesn't mean that nothing exists but that everything is interdependent. As a great Buddhist philosopher stated: "Because there's nothing that is not empty, therefore there is nothing that is not interdependent. Because there is nothing that is not interdependent, therefore there is nothing that is not empty in its nature."

There's nothing that doesn't depend on many things, nothing we can isolate. We call this a "hand" because it's connected to a whole body, otherwise it would just be a piece of flesh. We call this a "table" because it has four legs and a certain height, because there's a chair behind and different objects laid on it, otherwise we would call it a shelf or a plank or anything. Things seem to exist, but their existence is very relative. They only have a relative nature, no absolute nature. "Relative" means they depend on many things. Interdependence is therefore the closest way of describing their true nature.

The way things really are, their true nature, is there all the time. There's nothing to be "done" about it. It's not to be improved. It can't be damaged. The problem is not with the way things are; the problem is our own way of seeing things. We can't see the true nature, and therefore we have problems, so how can we develop a right way of seeing things? If we study things one by one, we won't understand their true nature because we separate things from one another, which prevents any real understanding. We're not doing some social research or intellectual investigation—that's not our purpose. Even a correct intellectual understanding of the true nature will be of no use, because it won't change the way we actually see things. What we're trying to do through the practice of Dharma is to change our whole approach completely. It's not a matter of exchanging one form, one concept, or one belief for another; that would just be a change of name, of label. Whether we say that everything is emptiness or that everything is real, both statements are just concepts. The real change comes only when we experientially see things as they really are.

This can happen only when we perceive directly, without ideas, without concepts. Is this possible? This work by Gampopa, *The Jewel Ornament of Liberation*, is the union of the Kadampa and the Mahamudra traditions. The Mahamudra is the highest, deepest Vajrayana teaching. How to see the truth directly, in a nonconceptual way, is precisely the real practice of Mahamudra. That's what we're coming to now.

To see things clearly, directly, in a nonconceptual way requires a lot of training because we're not used to such an approach. Whatever we feel, whatever comes up in our mind, we label it, brand it, register it;

we give it a name and assess it as good or bad, attractive or repulsive. We stamp everything. We build whole castles in the air. We make a big thing out of what was just a trifle. A car goes by in the street and there we go: "Oh, there's a car passing by. It's noisy. It's disturbing. I'm trying to meditate but how can I meditate with all these cars going up and down all the time! This is terrible!" We can go on like that for hours. If we just hear the sound and leave it there, everything's finished. This is just a small example of how we react all the time.

If we can see things as they are, there's no problem. We're liberated, we're buddhas! Our buddha nature is complete within us; we only have to discover it, to unfold it. What's to be disposed of are our own concepts and habitual patterns. These are what obstruct us. There's no one, no *mara*,[45] no devil with horns and fire putting obstacles in our way: we are obstructing ourselves. There's no obstruction but our own concepts, ideas, conditionings. To see through them is not beyond our power. We don't have to peel off layer after layer with sharp tools and drilling machines. All we have to change is our way of seeing things.

Gampopa says to illustrate this:

Now, since all phenomena are voidness itself, one may wonder whether or not it is necessary to cultivate this awareness. Indeed it is necessary. For instance, even though silver ore has the very nature of silver, the silver itself will not be apparent until the ore has been smelted and worked on.

We come to the actual practice. We won't be able to see things in a fresh and new way immediately. We'll first have to do some preliminaries, which means we'll have to exercise, tame, and train our mind so that it becomes relaxed, clearer, and quieter. We have to get rid of the hectic and tumultuous confusion, the turmoil and heavy smog that covers our mind. This can be done only through meditation, and this is why we need to meditate.

The text says: "These involve settling the mind into its natural, relaxed state."

Shamatha meditation is not something we make up; it simply

means relaxing in a natural way. We could talk about shamatha meditation for weeks, but actually it just means to relax in a natural way. It's not easy. We're so used to doing things in an artificial way that we encounter great difficulty in doing things naturally, or rather not "doing" anything. We sometimes think that "natural" means the way we usually do things, but that's not it. What we usually do is conditioned by our habits, culture, and confusion.

When we are completely relaxed, the tensions in our body and mind naturally diminish. We let our mind settle down and relax without "doing" things. If we sit thinking, "Am I relaxed now?" it isn't natural. Through regular practice, we'll get to know what is meant here. It's like learning to ride a bicycle. However good the teacher and the explanation may be, you have to learn by yourself. You may see others riding easily and feel jealous, wondering how they manage. You try once, twice, many times, and each time you fall. But there finally comes a moment when you're just able to do it. How nice! How did it happen? Of course, even then, you should be careful: there will be potholes and though you know you should avoid them, you just fall straight into them. It seems that this is how one learns, be it riding a bicycle or meditating.

The text quotes the *Prajnaparamita in Seven Hundred Verses:* "Dear sons, dear daughters! Rely on solitary meditation and delight in the absence of busyness. Sitting cross-legged and not projecting any specific notions, cultivate awareness and so forth . . ."

We're now going to discuss how to meditate in order to directly see the nature of our mind. We're all going to get enlightened today! Maybe you know the story of Milarepa's first encounter with the Dharma. He had asked a lama for instructions so as to practice the Dharma. The lama told him, "You're really lucky! You've knocked at the right door! I have a very strong and direct method. If you start to meditate in the morning, you'll get enlightened in the afternoon. If you start meditating in the afternoon, you'll get enlightened the next morning." Convinced that he was really lucky—because he had previously been immediately successful in studying black magic—Milarepa didn't bother to start practicing at once. A few days later, the lama came to inquire how he was doing. Milarepa told him that he hadn't even started, because he thought he could reach his goal any time. The lama then sighed and explained this wasn't what he had meant. He had to send him to another teacher because his instructions would now be useless for Milarepa. Let's avoid such a mistake!

The actual meditation has to be practiced according to the Mahamudra system of guidance: "One lets the mind settle free from even the slightest mental effort to posit, negate, adopt, or reject."

The mind settles down freely, completely free. That's the main point. Usually we're not free; we don't let our mind be free. We make concepts and comparisons; we brand and name and judge. We label, fix, and divide anything that comes to our mind. "This is this," "This it that," "This is mine," "This is yours." We never let our consciousness be completely free. If we just let things be as they are, without imposing anything on them, there's no effort. To compartmentalize, compare, posit and negate, adopt and reject, all these mental activities are a source of stress and strain. When we talk about the natural state of mind, we mean complete freedom without any restriction. This is called the union of shamatha and vipashyana, because the mind is at the same time calm and quiet, and we see directly into its depth, without being obstructed or veiled by efforts, thoughts, or activities.

This is exemplified by a quotation from Tilopa. Tilopa was the teacher of Naropa, who was Marpa's teacher, himself the teacher of Milarepa. One of the main siddhas of India, he's the first human link in the transmission lineage of the Mahamudra teachings. He earned his living by grinding sesame seeds (*tilo* in Sanskrit) to extract oil that he would sell to prostitutes, and it is while doing this that he attained realization. Here are the instructions he gave to Naropa: "Do not ponder, do not think, do not be aware, do not meditate, do not analyze—leave mind to itself."

"Do not ponder" translates a Tibetan expression that means one shouldn't follow thoughts or memories of the past, that one shouldn't dwell on past events. "Do not think" refers to the future, to planning, speculation, and anticipation. "Do not be aware" refers to the present. "Be aware" is the usual instruction for the beginner's meditation, but at a higher level, trying to be aware is an effort, and even the effort of remaining aware should be left behind. Of course, this doesn't mean that we shouldn't try to maintain awareness while we're still in the first phase of developing shamatha meditation: if we don't develop awareness as beginners, we may quickly find ourselves in Mexico or anywhere! "Do not meditate" means that we shouldn't make any effort to meditate. If we "try" to meditate, we constrict our mind into a structure so that it fits our concept of "meditation." We can even say such things as "Now my meditation is lost" or "I can't meditate anymore." This kind of cultivation of meditation is not appropriate within the Mahamudra approach. "Do not analyze" also means that we should let ourselves be completely free. Of course, analysis is very important in the beginning. If our mind is unable to settle down, if we experience strong emotions or have a very solid view of reality, we have to use reason, logic, analysis to dismantle this grasping at things. But these are only means toward a higher stage. When we really want to see the truth in a direct way, even these methods that are usually considered good and important become obstructive and should be discarded. "Leave mind to itself" means we should remain completely natural, without any contrivance, without adding or suppressing anything. These are the six methods of Tilopa to realize what is sometimes called the "ordinary mind" or the "spontaneous wisdom."

Other quotations follow to explain the above. One is from Saraha, one of the earliest exponents of Vajrayana Buddhism in India. He composed many *dohas*, which are songs of realization. Sometimes poems or songs come up in the mind of those who realize the truth, as a spontaneous expression of their joy and experience. Some of Saraha's dohas are so beautiful that they've become folk songs. Some of them are still sung nowadays by farmers in certain regions in India although they have no idea of what they actually mean. "Listen, child! Whatever thoughts you may have, within this state of rest, there's no one bound, no one free. Therefore, O joy! Shedding your fatigue, rest naturally, without contrivance or distraction."

What's binding us are our concepts, the contriving framework that we're constantly building up. If we weren't creating all this, there would be nothing binding us, nothing to free ourselves from. Saraha has discovered that we've never been bound in the first place. We've always been free: there's complete openness and therefore complete joy; there's nothing to worry about, nothing to think or ponder, no limitations—it's complete rest. Saraha understood that he had been confused, that he had needlessly limited and burdened himself and that all his suffering had been totally useless. Nothing had ever bound him; he had always been perfectly free. Realizing this, he had gained perfect rest and happiness. Gampopa also gives two quotations from Nagarjuna:

> An elephant that has been trained, like a mind that has entered a relaxed state, has stopped running to and fro and (remains) naturally calm. Thus have I realized, and hence what need do I have of a teaching?
>
> Don't adopt an attitude or think in any way whatsoever. Don't interfere or contrive but leave mind loose in its own nature. The uncontrived is the unborn true nature. This is to follow in the wake of all the enlightened ones of the three times.

The most important word in this quotation is "uncontrived." If the mind is uncontrived, it remains in its natural state. This is the state of mind of the buddhas of the past, the future, and the present. If we can let our mind be completely natural, we'll see the truth and experience complete rest and freedom. This is something that happens naturally. Another great siddha, Shawaripa, said:

> Do not see faults anywhere. Practice that which is nothing whatsoever. Do not foster longing for signs of progress and the like. Although it is taught that there is nothing whatsoever to meditate on, do not fall under the sway of inactivity and indifference. In all circumstances, practice with mindfulness.

This is also very important. So far, we've emphasized that there's nothing to meditate on, nothing to do, that we should give up all activities, concepts, and contrivance. However, if we interpret this as an excuse for sleeping all day long, we'll never see the true nature of our mind either: we'll remain in our usual conditioned state as slaves of our habitual tendencies. Although there's nothing to meditate on, we should remain in the meditation, we should constantly be in that free, natural, uncontrived state and familiarize ourselves with it.

Even if we get a glimpse of insight into the true nature of the mind, if we don't familiarize ourselves with it, we'll lose that experience. There is a Tibetan saying that goes something like "The Dharma has no self, but whoever has the biggest self (in terms of determination, endurance, willpower, and perseverance) gets the result." Of course, this is a joke, a pun impossible to translate accurately into English, but in a way it's quite true. You probably know the story of the last and most important teaching of Milarepa to Gampopa. This is a story I like very much. When Gampopa had to leave Milarepa to practice on his own, Milarepa accompanied him to see him off until they came to a small brook he wouldn't cross. He said to Gampopa, "Now you go. We may not see each other again, but it doesn't matter. However, there's a most precious instruction that I haven't given you yet. Still maybe I shouldn't give it to you. It's too precious." However much Gampopa pleaded to receive it, Milarepa refused. Gampopa sadly walked away. He hadn't gone very far when Milarepa suddenly called him back: "If I don't give it to you, who will ever deserve to receive it? You're my best student." Gampopa prostrated several times, offered a mandala, and formally requested this pith instruction. Milarepa then turned around, pulled up his clothes, and showed Gampopa his bottom, saying, "This is my last and most important instruction!" His bottom was full of scars and hard as rock because of all the years he spent sitting in meditation. The message is the same: even if there's "nothing" to meditate on, we have to work very hard!

We have now seen the meditation techniques through which we

may come to experience the basic or "ordinary" natural state of our mind. To see our consciousness or mind without any confusion or delusion, without the constructs we cover it with, is to see the truth. This is regarded as the very heart, the essence, of meditation.

In Buddhism, there are only two kinds of meditation. The first is the stabilization meditation, shamatha, which makes our minds calm and clear. The second and more important is vipashyana, which is all about insight, seeing the truth, getting a direct realization. Through this meditation, we see the true nature of our consciousness directly, nakedly, without veils. If we have this realization, all the other paramitas become transcendent.

How to Integrate Wisdom   How do we carry this view into our everyday life, when we're not meditating? We can't remain in meditation all the time. Whether we had true realization, a fleeting experience or a short-lived glimpse of insight, how does it affect our daily life, during the postmeditation period? "Postmeditation" is how the Tibetan word is usually translated, but Ken Holmes uses the term "intermeditation phase," which I find a good idea, as it suggests that we'll meditate again, whereas "postmeditation" has no such implication.

Gampopa says: "While viewing everything that occurs in between (meditation sessions) as illusory, one should establish every wholesome merit one can, through the practice of generosity and so forth."

Sometimes, when we've gained a little bit of understanding, when we've had a fleeting, unstable experience of seeing the true nature, we come to think that there's nothing, that everything's empty, that there's no good, no evil, no heaven, no hell, no karma, nothing. When this kind of view is translated into our daily life, what happens is that we belittle or even ignore the relative truth, thereby making mistakes of which we will bear the negative results. When we neglect the relative aspect of things, all kinds of trouble may ensue. Even if our meditation is very high, even if we clearly see everything as illusory, we should be very careful with our actions, our speech, and our mind. The situations we experience, the world we live in, depend on actions and reactions at a relative level. Even if they are illusory, events happen and affect us. Life may be like a dream, but as long as we're still dreaming, we're affected by what happens in our dream. This is why, during the inter-meditation phases, we should try to carry on the understanding gained during the meditation; we should try to rest our mind in its true nature, but with a clear discursive awareness so as to tell right from wrong and harmonize our actions accordingly.

As we can see if we look around us, there are many different kinds of people. Some can do a lot without being too stressed and overwhelmed, whereas others can't even do one or two things without feeling it's too much, too heavy, too difficult. It all depends on how we manage our daily life. Most of the time, we carry what we have to do in our mind like a burden. I know what I'm talking about, as I often do this myself. For instance, I receive a letter and think, "I'll answer tomorrow." The next day, I receive two or three other letters and think, "OK, I'll answer them all together tomorrow." After a month, I have a pile of unanswered letters, and I postpone it every day because it has become too heavy. I could have answered each letter within a minute the moment I received it. In the same way, it's not the work in itself that generates stress but our approach to what we have to do. We make a big deal out of little things, carry them as heavy burdens, and regard most of what we have to do as difficult and unpleasant. Thinking about what we still have to do prevents us from actually doing it, because we already feel so busy: we worry about all that we haven't done yet instead of doing it. When we've gained some meditative understanding, it's recommended to recollect this understanding within our daily activities and remain under its influence. It will enable us to feel free and light, to take things as they come. We can then accomplish whatever has to be done without getting too attached to what we do or to the eventual results of our action. If things come out all right, it's good. If they don't, so be it. If we can cultivate such an attitude, we'll be able to do many things without feeling overburdened. We should also try to do as many positive things as possible. Our discursive awareness will allow us to distinguish right from wrong, for ourselves as well as for others, and we'll be able to manage things in a way that doesn't weigh heavily on our mind.

If we're able to carry our practice along with us in our daily life, there's no need to abandon our relative world and our worldly responsibilities. It will remain possible for us to carry our practice and meditation along with a very busy life full of responsibilities. This is precisely the Vajrayana approach!

It's said that the whole of the Buddhist path is included in the understanding of the true nature of mind and phenomena. Be it refuge, bodhichitta, the six paramitas, offerings, virtuous deeds, prostrations, purification; the observance of commitments, precepts, and vows; study, contemplation and meditation, everything is included in it, as the different excerpts from the sutras quoted by Gampopa illustrate. For instance, regarding refuge, Gampopa quotes *The Sutra Requested by the King of the Naga, Anavatapta:*[46]

> Bodhisattvas are aware that every phenomenon is without entity, without being, without life, and without personality. To see in the way the Tathagatas see—not as forms, not as names, and not as specific phenomena—that is to have taken refuge in the Buddha with a mind unpolluted by materialism.

How to integrate the understanding of the true nature of phenomena into all activities is abundantly exemplified, but I won't go into more details. I would, however, advise you to read this section carefully.

Certain types of meditation make use of yogic techniques that work on the mind through the medium of the body. Mental states are very volatile and unstable. What we call our personality is not a set of fixed characteristics that we carry on throughout our whole life. It's highly changeable. Body and mind, like everything else, depend on each other. Mental states can affect the body, and physical states can alter the mind and lead to "personality" modifications. The body can change to the point that there's no mind anymore: that's when we die! This shows the very close connection between body and mind—at least at its grosser levels. This connection is very important and has been acknowledged for a very long time. In Tibetan medicine, it's well known that a bile excess will cause the patient to get angry easily and that too much wind can drive someone crazy; the treatment will consist in correcting the physical imbalance. Yogic exercises also correspond to a conscious effort to control the mind through control of the body. One can't say that mind is "producing" matter or that matter is "producing" mind, as some modern scientists believe. We aren't, however, interested in entering into a scientific discussion because what matters to us, what Buddhists are concerned with, is how to deal with the situations we encounter daily, how to get rid of suffering and find peace of mind and happiness. In this particular context, mind becomes much more important than matter, because happiness and unhappiness are both mental states depending on how our mind reacts. Confronted with the same situation, different mental reaction will make one person happy and another unhappy. I'm not saying that matter is nonexistent or that it plays no part in the situation. Matter and mind are interdependent. Mind is as real as matter, or we could rather say that matter is as unreal as mind, and both are very powerful, but mind being our subjective perception of our world, it's something we can alter and control. The purpose of all the different practices of Buddhism, be it the different kinds of meditation, visualizations, *yidam* and sadhana practices, or even the observance of precepts, is geared toward setting our mind free of all concepts, habits, and conditionings. The objective is to get our mind to directly see its true nature, because this is the most powerful way to liberate ourselves. It clears away all delusions, barriers, and confusion.

There has always been great debate as to whether this realization is sudden or gradual. In a way, it's sudden. Seeing—having a direct experience of something—can't be gradual. When we open a window, we immediately, suddenly see everything that's out there. The landscape isn't disclosed gradually. In the same way, one experiences the natural mind in a flash, suddenly. However, this doesn't mean that we can't build up our understanding. We first have to learn and thereby develop more confidence. As it becomes clearer and clearer, we may one day have the sudden experience of it. In the beginning, this experience may come and go. It's unstable. Then slowly—or quickly, according to the individual—we may stabilize the experience. It's believed that even though we may directly see the true nature of our mind almost constantly whenever we meditate, we may remain unable to carry on this experience within our normal life. This is the meaning of Milarepa's last instruction: we have to constantly practice and train in order to clarify, deepen, and stabilize our experience. This is also why Gampopa later talks about the different bhumis, the different levels of attainment. Our habitual patterns and tendencies are very strong, and even with a stable direct experience and though we may have overcome most of our negative emotions and confusion, still some of our habitual conditionings may remain for a long time. This is why we need to be very diligent.

Results and Benefits   We now come to the signs of development, the signs that show whether we've been meditating and practicing correctly or not. This is the evaluation, the test of our practice and understanding. "The signs of prajna's development are increased attention to virtue, a diminution of defilement, the arising of compassion for sentient beings, earnest application to practice, rejection of all distraction, and no more attachment to or craving for the things of this life."

All our practices have to diminish our negative emotions. If they don't, it means they're no good! We should examine whether we've become less angry, less proud, less jealous, whether we cling less to things. We may have received countless teachings from a hundred high lamas for the past twenty years, stayed in retreat locked in a cave for twelve years, been practicing every day beating a drum and chanting from morning to night, but what does it all matter if we haven't subdued our negative emotions? What really matters is how much we have effectively worked on ourselves. If we were angry people and have become less angry, this means we've really done something. That's the real practice, whatever our formal practice may have been. It doesn't even matter whether it was a "Buddhist" practice or not. How much we managed to lessen our negative emotions is the real sign of positive development, which testifies to a correct approach of spiritual practice.

The second sign is that we've become more compassionate. This is a natural development. If we work on our negative emotions, we become naturally more aware of the other's problems than our own. When we've gained some understanding and clarity regarding the true nature of what we are, it's completely natural to feel greater compassion because we've become less selfish, less self-centered.

There are many other signs, but in fact they're all included in these two: our negative emotions diminish and our compassion grows. They mean that we're on the right path.

What also naturally happens, although it's not mentioned in the text, is that we become more joyful. One of the good signs of correct Dharma practice is that the practitioner becomes easier to live with. If we flare up in irritation and anger at the slightest provocation, it means we still have to work hard. We should become less easy to provoke. If someone says something rather nasty to us and we don't take it too seriously, that's a good sign. We usually get angry very easily. If we let this habit grow, we'll end up considering everybody an enemy and feeling that everything out there is ready to harm us. We'll get completely paranoid. If we become only a little less self-centered, a little more compassionate, we'll feel freer, more relaxed and joyful, and therefore easier to live with. This is already a great act of compassion because we're actually helping ourselves as well as others. When we talk of "working for the benefit of all sentient beings," it sounds very nice, but who are these "sentient beings"? Where are they? There may be billions of sentient beings all over the world and the universe, but most important are those close to us. If I generate compassionate thoughts for "all sentient beings" but feel very angry with some members of my family or keep a burning hatred for one of my neighbors, my "universal compassion" doesn't sound very genuine, does it? Kindness and working for the benefit of all sentient beings start with ourselves and the people next to us. If we're kind to the person next to us, this kindness will extend from that person to the next, and so on. This is how we should work with the world. How can we pretend to wish that all beings be happy if we can't even be nice to our neighbors?

The ultimate result of the practice of wisdom is to get enlightened, to reach buddhahood. The temporary, relative result is to feel joy and delight while still residing in samsara.

THE FIVE LEVELS OF THE BODHISATTVA PATH

From one point of view, it is not necessary to know beforehand the different levels that delineate the path toward enlightenment. We only need to practice regularly and see what happens. However, it's only natural to want to know where we are, to evaluate the distance already covered, and to know what still lies ahead. Without a sense of the whole journey, we risk making mistakes or feeling lost and confused. Some might think that they've achieved something great when they only had a small experience or gained some little understanding. Others risk getting discouraged seeing years go by without having obtained what they felt was so easily within reach. If we know that the path is long and has several levels, we'll be less impatient and will not expect to get enlightened quickly and without effort. We'll become aware of the depth of the problems we face. We only have to think of the difficulties encountered by those who attempt to solve problems stemming from their childhood: the lengthy therapies and treatments, the energy and willpower required. . . . But here we're talking about complete freedom, about liberating ourselves from all the extremely deep and powerful conditionings that have been created and reinforced over so many lifetimes! We can't expect to free ourselves easily of such conditioning. We have to dive into the very depths of our mind, to the very root of our psyche. We have to go very deep because the problem is very deeply rooted. This is not easy.

However, this doesn't mean that solving these problems will necessarily take a long time. The time required depends on each individual person's capacity, but time isn't the essential factor. What is essential is to go directly to the deepest level of consciousness, deeper than that reached through any kind of therapy and, once it is reached, to purify it of all its conditionings.

If this objective is not understood correctly, we may meditate for months, for years, or for our whole lives without obtaining the slightest result. We must become aware that this task isn't easy; otherwise we'll soon become discouraged when we see that little has changed and that our problems persist after several months or years of practice. Gampopa has condensed what we call the thirty-seven branches of enlightenment into five phases.

1. Accumulation

The first phase of the path is that of accumulation. At this stage, we're just beginning and gathering as many positive actions as possible. We may not have perfect virtue or wisdom, but we do our best and aim toward it. We strive to develop compassion, bodhichitta, and virtue, through study, reflection, and meditation. We work at this with enthusiasm and regularity, and little by little we notice progress.

Gampopa included twelve of the thirty-seven branches of enlightenment in this phase, notably the Four Trainings in Mindfulness, the Four Right Practices, and the Four Supports of Miraculous Manifestation.

The path begins from the moment we have generated bodhichitta by expressing the wish to become a buddha and to help all beings do likewise. Through making this aspiration we dedicate ourselves to following the path of enlightened beings. Until we have focused on a specific destination, we wander aimlessly. Even if we walk for miles in a particular direction, we can't claim to have begun the journey. On the other hand, from the moment we've decided to get somewhere, even if we should take the opposite direction, our journey has already begun. As soon as bodhichitta has arisen in our minds and we make positive efforts to develop it further, we're traveling the path of enlightened beings.

When we're at the stage of accumulation, we must do everything we can to stay on the right path, by listening, reflecting, meditating, and practicing. At this level, we still lack confidence and faith because we don't have a direct insight into the real nature of things yet. We may still have doubts, and this is normal, but we must try to eliminate them with our intelligence, through deduction, logic, and reasoning. It's also essential to find a teacher we can trust. We need reliable teachings on which to base our convictions, our philosophy, and our lifestyle. Our way of life then becomes the path.

2. Integration

The second phase is what we call the phase of integration, or some-times the stage of junction. We're ready to take stock of what we've learned and acquired. This phase, which is divided into four subphases, traces the fine line between the samsaric state of mind of ordinary be-ings and the nonsamsaric state of mind of higher beings. It's therefore an intermediate phase, for some lasting only a few moments and for others several months or years, but it is nevertheless a relatively short period of time. We could say that it's the summit of the accumulation phase that precedes access to the next phase. As we move closer to the latter we perceive its warmth and develop an increased confidence. This is why the first subphase is called "warming." It's as if a fire were close by, hidden by a curtain: we can't see it, but it's so close that we can feel its heat and we're sure of its presence. Our meditation, our under-standing, and our confidence are so strong that nearly all our doubts disappear. Then come the subphases of the "summit" and "forbear-ance." The last subphase is called "the highest worldly point." It's the last stage at which we still retain a samsaric view of things.

Gampopa explains that if we relate this phase to the thirty-seven branches of enlightenment, emphasis is placed on the practice of the five faculties and the five powers.

3. Insight

The third phase is that of insight, the direct experience of truth and the real nature of mind, the stage of Mahamudra. Here one obtains the state of an arya, which means "raised above." Although not yet a perfect buddha, one is nevertheless no longer a samsaric being.

When we speak of the view, it isn't really a matter of seeing in the usual sense, but rather "experiencing directly." At this stage, we have access to the complete experience of the truth. There's no higher view, which doesn't mean, however, that it can't be widened, deepened, or improved upon. There are many philosophical debates on this point. According to some, as the view is an experience of the truth in its totality, it can't have gradations within it. Others argue that there are gradations and higher levels. The latter illustrate their point of view with the following example: someone in a dark room who sees the sky through a small keyhole really does see the sky but doesn't know what the whole sky looks like, with stars, clouds, the horizon, and so on. Similarly, one can have seen the truth without having experienced it extensively. The more we progress, the more our view widens and deepens. The keyhole becomes a window, then a bay window, until all partitions disappear and we find ourselves outside on a beach, where at last we can see the sky in its totality.

This third phase corresponds to the first bhumi of the bodhisattva levels, as well as to the level of the "stream enterer" in the Theravada tradition.

4. Meditation

The fourth phase is that of cultivation or meditation. We have of course practiced meditation before reaching this stage, but up to this point our meditation has remained worldly. It's only at the fourth phase that one can speak of transcendental meditation, or of the paramita of meditation.

As soon as we've reached the stage of the view, we're liberated from confusion and illusion. Nevertheless, our habits die hard. It's very difficult to get rid of them, and this fourth phase, itself subdivided into ten different stages, records our progressive elimination of these habitual tendencies. These different levels, or bhumis, of a bodhisattva will be explained in detail in the following section. In the beginning, everything is clear while we're meditating, but confusion returns as soon as we come out of meditation. As we progress through the stages, the line between meditation and postmeditation softens until it finally disappears.

It is at this stage that we are endowed with the eightfold path of the Realized.

5. Complete Accomplishment

The fifth phase is that of complete accomplishment. This is sometimes referred to as the phase "beyond meditation" or "beyond study." In this final stage, we've become fully awakened buddhas, we've nothing further to accomplish, and there's no longer any difference between meditation and daily life. Milarepa attained this stage, sometimes referred to as the "yoga of the flowing river": no matter what we do, the river keeps flowing. In this phase there's nothing that is not meditation. We're in permanent meditation, without a trace of confusion and with nothing that can trouble us. We also speak of "vajralike samadhi." According to the Indian legend, the vajra is a bone so hard that it is indestructible. It can destroy or break through anything without itself being destroyed. Remaining in a "vajralike" meditation means that nothing can destroy, trouble, or impede our meditation; we are unshakable.

Gampopa lists the five qualities of this vajralike meditation:

> It is unimpeded since no worldly activity can be a cause that might unsettle it; it is durable since none of the obscurations can damage it; it is stable since no thought can trouble it; it is homogenous since it is of one taste; and it is all pervading since it is focused upon the ultimate nature common to each and every thing that is knowable.

THE TEN BODHISATTVA LEVELS

The ten bodhisattva levels, also known as the ten bhumis, correspond to the fourth phase, that of cultivation or meditation, which is divided here into ten levels. The path therefore comprises thirteen levels: the beginner's level, the level of practice born of aspiration, the ten bodhisattva levels, and the level of buddhahood.

What we're discussing now are the experiences of the bodhisattvas themselves. We haven't yet achieved these levels and know nothing of them. We can't speculate much about them and can only listen to how realized beings describe their experiences to us. This chapter gives us an idea of what would happen if we chanced to really practice assiduously.

This can also give us an idea of where we stand now. We can go through many different experiences during our practice. In fact, there's nothing we can't experience in meditation. Sometimes we can feel we are the worst of the worst, the dumbest and lowest of all, whereas at other times we can feel we are the highest of the highest, like a completely awakened buddha. None of these experiences, called *nyam* in Tibetan, are real. They're fleeting and temporary. If we overlook this, we can imagine having reached perfect realization, start acting accordingly, and make many mistakes, which can have disastrous consequences, both for ourselves and for those around us. It's in order to avoid these painful situations that we detail the different phases and all the stages they include.

On the other hand, listing them can discourage some. The spiritual path, made up of so many phases and levels, can seem too long and difficult for us. However, we should remember that for anyone who has reached the first bhumi, time no longer has any real importance. A real bodhisattva no longer has any problems, as the verses of the *Bodhicharyavatara* I already quoted explain: "By the virtue of merit, the body is at ease; by the virtue of wisdom, the mind is at ease; therefore, however long a bodhisattva remains in samsara, he is never unhappy."

Once we have this little bit of wisdom, once we've experienced the true nature of phenomena, the mind becomes peaceful and free of any attachment or grasping. We've stopped chasing after or running away from things. No longer subject to suffering and unhappiness, we remain content, joyful, and relaxed. We no longer mind remaining in samsara. Our mind and actions are pure. In fact, a pure mind can't commit negative actions.

As positive actions necessarily bring positive karmic consequences, bodhisattvas don't experience real suffering. Even if they choose to be born in a very ordinary form, in a difficult environment where there is a lot of suffering, they may outwardly experience the laws of interdependence and undergo many trials, but at the inner level of the mind, the level that really counts, they don't experience suffering.

Such bodhisattvas can choose to stay in the world a very long time without being disturbed by it. They remain in the world in order to help others. Becoming a buddha doesn't mean that one ceases to help others; on the contrary, one's capacity to help increases infinitely, but to become a buddha is no longer a bodhisattva's priority.

Gampopa describes in detail the ten bodhisattva levels, their nature, their meaning, their birthplace, and the particular mastery and purity as well as the particular practice associated with each. I don't think it necessary to go into such detail, so we'll look at a summary of each bhumi.

The first bhumi is named Supreme Joy. This level is described as follows: "Upon seeing that enlightenment is close and that the good of beings is accomplished, there will arise the most supreme joy. For that reason it is called Supreme Joy."

Those who reach this stage experience great joy. Enlightenment is within their reach, and their actions are of real benefit to others. Their constant joy stems from a conviction that the samsaric state of mind is behind them and that from now on they will be able to help all beings. At this stage, all the confusion and defilements caused by lack of understanding are completely purified and eliminated.

However, other forms of negativity such as deeply rooted habits and tendencies are not so easy to erase. Taking the example of an onion, one could say that only the first skin has been removed. Bodhisattvas at this level practice all six paramitas, but they have perfected the first paramita of generosity.

Gampopa describes the particular abilities connected to this first bhumi as follows. One can:

1. Attain one hundred profound absorptions and experience their stable fruition,
2. See one hundred buddhas,
3. Most properly be aware of those buddhas' blessings,
4. Shake one hundred world systems,
5. Visit one hundred buddhafields,
6. Illuminate one hundred world systems,
7. Bring one hundred sentient beings to full maturity,
8. Live for one hundred eons,
9. Be excellently aware of the past and future up to one hundred eons past or hence,
10. Open one hundred gates of Dharma,
11. Manifest one hundred emanations anywhere, and
12. Manifest each of these physical forms as being accompanied by one hundred other bodhisattvas.

These particular abilities are multiplied at each bhumi.

The second bhumi is called Immaculate. "This level is known as Immaculate since it is unstained by violations of right conduct." At this level, the practice of the paramita of right conduct is mastered and becomes transcendent, being brought to its highest point.

The third bhumi is called Illuminator. "It is known as the Illuminator because in that state the light of Dharma and profound absorption is very clear; furthermore, it illuminates others with the great light of Dharma." It's the practice of the paramita of forbearance that becomes transcendent.

The fourth bhumi is called Radiant. "It is called Radiant because the brilliance of primordial wisdom, endowed with the qualities favorable

to enlightenment, radiates everywhere and has consumed the two obscurations." Here it's the practice of the paramita of diligence that
becomes transcendent.

The fifth bhumi is called Difficult to Practice, because at this level
wisdom hasn't been totally realized, and so we still encounter difficulties in the practice of the prajnaparamita. "On this level one strives to
help beings achieve some maturity yet transcend any defiled reaction
to their repeated mistakes. It is known as Difficult to Practice because
both (helping and not reacting) are hard to master." One hasn't yet
reached a perfect realization of nonduality. Because of this, when one
tries to help others and the result is not as expected, one worries—for
example, when all beings fail to get enlightened. The word "difficult" is
used because we're on the point of reaching a totally nondualistic view
but still have some traces of duality. After this level, everything seems
very easy. At this stage, one has perfected the paramita of meditation.

The sixth bhumi is called Revealed. "Due to the support of prajnaparamita there is no dwelling on (notions of) either nirvana or samsara. Thus, samsara and nirvana are revealed as pure." At this level, the
sixth paramita of wisdom is perfectly realized. There's no more duality.
The dualistic approach of seeing nirvana as good and samsara as bad
disappears so that nothing impure remains in our perspective. All
truths are thus revealed.

The seventh bhumi is Far Gone. "This level is known as Far Gone
since it connects with the 'one and only path' and one has come to the
far end of activity." The nonseparateness of everything is realized at
this level. All the various characteristics of Dharma, the sutras and so
forth, don't appear as separate. One no longer sees anything as separate. From this level onward, our most subtle habitual patterns and
tendencies begin to fade away.

The eighth bhumi is called Immovable. "It is so called because it is
unmoved by ideas that either strive after characteristics or strive after
an absence of characteristics."

One acquires what we call the "ten powers" over (1) lifespan, (2) mind, (3) commodities, (4) action, (5) birth state, (6) prayer, (7) intentions, (8) miracles, (9) primordial wisdom, and (10) Buddhadharma.

The ninth bhumi is called Excellent Intelligence or Perfect Discernment. "That level is Excellent Intelligence because of its good intelligence, clearly discerning. . . . It is achieved through twelve factors such as infinite prayers. . . . Although bodhisattvas on this level practice all ten paramitas in general, it is said that they place particular emphasis on that of powers."

The tenth bhumi is called Cloud of Dharma. "It is called Cloud of Dharma because the bodhisattvas on that level are like a cloud that causes a rain of Dharma teachings to fall upon beings, thereby washing away the fine dust of their defilements." A cloud doesn't ponder, "Shall I rain or not? Do this earth and these people beneath me want my rain? Do they deserve it?" No, a cloud simply sheds its rain. In the same way, at this level, everything is accomplished in the natural order of things; whatever is to be done is done spontaneously.

The last bhumi corresponds to the state of buddhahood, the fifth phase discussed in the previous section. "This corresponds to the stage that is the Phase of Completion. When the vajralike profound absorption arises, it eliminates simultaneously the obscurations to be removed by (the phase of) cultivation." At this level, all obstacles and problems due to our mind poisons, disturbing emotions, and habitual patterns are completely purified. Our compassion and virtue have fully blossomed. We have nothing more to do and nothing further to develop. This is the buddha level.

5. THE RESULT:
Perfect Buddhahood

We now reach the chapter that deals with the state of buddhahood and its different aspects.

Discussing this subject is even more difficult than presenting the phases that lead to it. Indeed none of us knows what buddhahood is really like, and after reading the last chapter it can seem a long way off! Reaching buddhahood can indeed take a very long time. The *Bodhisattvabhumi* states, "These levels are accomplished over the span of three countless cosmic eons." However, the phases we've just covered don't necessarily take a long time; what matters is not the time but the approach we take. The main point is to be able to get a direct realization of our true nature and then get rid of our habitual patterns. Working on these habitual tendencies takes a very long time if we approach the path according to the usual Sutrayana way.

However, the unique Vajrayana path enables us to attain buddhahood in a single lifetime as long as we have the right conditions, the right mental attitude, the right understanding, and a qualified mentor who can transmit the strong, direct teachings that introduce us to the nature of mind, and provided that we work one-pointedly on this path. It is then possible to get enlightened in this very life, and it has been proven. The best example of such an achievement is Milarepa. Some of his disciples were persuaded that his level of accomplishment was such that he must be the reincarnation of a very great being. Milarepa replied that although they meant to be very respectful, even flattering, they were in fact belittling and underestimating the power of the Dharma. "You seem to be saying that one achieves nothing simply through practicing the Dharma and that, to get results, one must have been a very great person in past lives. However, I was nothing in particular in my previous life. What I am and what I have achieved is purely the fruit of my practice in this life!"

Gampopa describes seven aspects of buddhahood.

THE NATURE OF BUDDHAHOOD

First, the nature of buddhahood: "A truly perfect Buddha is the best possible purity and the best possible primordial wisdom (jnana)." A buddha has purified everything that needed to be purified and has awakened all the wisdom that needed to be awakened. All beings, whether human or nonhuman, have this potential, this essentially pure nature, hidden beneath their confusion and ignorance. In order to rediscover this original inner purity, we have to awaken the wisdom that's within us; this naturally purifies all our negativity, confusion, and ignorance.

These two aspects, the purification of negativity and the awakening of wisdom, are essentially one and the same thing. In fact, as soon as our true nature is awakened, our confusion and negativity are automatically purified. One becomes a buddha when this process has been perfectly accomplished. The different phases on the bodhisattva path correspond to levels of purification and the simultaneous awakening of wisdom.

Buddhist intellectuals have always held lively debates as to whether a buddha's wisdom has anything to do with our minds as they are now or whether it is something completely different. How can buddhas recognize things if they don't have the same vision as we? In fact, all the Buddhist philosophers agree that the essential characteristic of a buddha's mind is its nonconceptual, nondualistic quality. Buddhas have totally eliminated conceptuality and have transcended the dualistic approach that distinguishes between "me" and "other." When the mind of a buddha is described in this way, many people get a wrong idea and think that a state of mind devoid of concepts and duality must be like deep sleep or a kind of coma. As we don't know what such a state may be like, we can only imagine it as a total lack of awareness. This is not right, which is why we refer to this state as *jnana,* or primordial wisdom. Even in the absence of concepts and duality, it's not blank, but completely clear. As we discussed previously, concepts don't correspond to reality. As soon as we create a concept, we add to or subtract from what's really there. Concepts almost never reflect accurately what is. "Nonconceptual" means leaving things as they are, without adding or removing anything.

"Nonduality" has almost the same meaning. To say "This is my thought" or "This is disturbing me" reflects a dualistic approach. The sound of a car disturbing me implies that I posit the existence of an "I" that is disturbed when hearing a "noise." Who actually hears the noise? Is the noise separate from the person who hears it or not? If the noise and the hearer can't be separated, then how can I be disturbed by it? How can the sound disturb me if I'm not separate from it? This could only be the case if I think that there is something or someone distinct from the sound. If we can remain in a state of mind in which we do not differentiate between the sound and ourselves, we'll no longer be disturbed by noises, no matter how many cars go by.

A Zen story describes a scene in which a master and student are meditating together. Rain is falling, and its sound disturbs the student. The master tells him, "Just be one with the rain, then it can't possibly disturb you."

Saying that a buddha's wisdom is nondualistic doesn't mean that he no longer has any kind of understanding or cognition of what's going on around him, that he doesn't hear, see, or feel anything. It's in fact the exact opposite. A buddha feels, sees, and understands with much more clarity than we do. Our perception of things is constantly confused, because of the various concepts that we attach to them. As a buddha's mind has no duality, he has no feeling of separateness, hence he hasn't any feeling of aversion or attachment to anything. A buddha remains in a state of perfect equanimity. His mind is sharp and distinctive; he chases nothing nor runs away from anything. This is what we call wisdom.

In the light of this nondualistic and nonconceptual consciousness, our negative emotions are seen to be wisdom. One could say that wisdom is hidden beneath the negative emotions. As soon as our dualistic and conceptual way of seeing is dissipated, the Buddha's wisdom is revealed to our present consciousness. Emotions and perceptions of things are precisely the wisdom of the Buddha. Of course we don't have direct access to or complete understanding of this wisdom yet, since everything we think can only take the shape of our concepts, but we can nevertheless imagine what this experience could be like.

According to Milarepa:

> One talks of jnana, yet in itself it is uncontrived awareness, beyond all such terms as "is" or "is not," "eternal" or "nothing"; it is quite beyond the scope of the intellect. Therefore, no matter which terms are used to express it, there is nothing to refute. It is whatever it is. Some would-be scholars once asked Lord Buddha himself (about this topic) but his reply was: "Do not think there is any one-sided reply to this! Dharmakaya is beyond the grasp of the intellect. It is unborn and free of conceptual complication. Do not ask me; look into the mind. That is the way it is."

That's exactly it. Statements like "This must be like this or like that" are per se erroneous. What we think, whatever we grasp with our intellect, are just concepts, images we create in our mind; they're not the real thing. Seeing things as a buddha sees them implies that we don't think or decide intellectually or philosophically that "it must be like this or like that." It is something we have to experience. One of the main problems for human beings is their propensity to intellectualize everything. Before we practice something we want to understand it. This is a major obstacle to practice, at least at the level of seeing ultimate truth. We have doubts if we don't understand what we're doing, and some think that it's impossible to practice something that we don't understand. However, the message is: "Look into your mind. Don't conceptualize it. Then you may see." This is why we previously discussed the six methods of Tilopa, this direct, natural, uncontrived way of looking at ourselves that is the only method that enables us to discover our true nature. This is very difficult because we're not used to it. We always try to conceptualize things before acting. In this way we may be able to do many things, such as making airplanes or even atomic bombs, but we won't be able to see our true nature. As soon as we conceptualize something, we can no longer see its real essence. When we realize that our usual approach is simply not working, we feel lost, disconcerted, and unsure what to do. The only way is "to be." This is why the Buddha said, "Don't ask me; look into your mind." He could have given many answers, but none would have been complete or correct, because it is impossible to define, describe, or grasp the truth through the intellect.

ETYMOLOGY OF THE TERM *BUDDHA*

The second aspect of buddhahood lies in the etymology of the word *buddha*. "Why Buddha? The term *buddha*—'awakened plenitude'—is applied because they have awoken from sleeplike ignorance and because the mind has expanded to embrace the two aspects of the knowable." This is the etymology of *sang gye*, the Tibetan word for "buddha."

Sang means "awaken," and *gye* means "blossomed," "to open like a flower." *Sang gye* means "the one who has awoken from the sleep of ignorance and whose wisdom has blossomed and opened completely to embrace the two aspects of compassion and wisdom." In Sanskrit, *bodh* means "to awaken," "to realize," or "to see things clearly."

THE THREE KAYAS

The five other aspects of buddhahood are linked to the three kayas.

It is impossible to describe in a simple way what a buddha is. To be thorough, we have to approach a buddha from various angles, which then renders his different qualities intellectually accessible. The kayas are not different things but aspects of the same reality.

Most often we speak of three kayas: the dharmakaya, the sambhogakaya, and the nirmanakaya. When reference is made to two kayas, they are the dharmakaya and the *rupakaya*. *Rupakaya* means "form body" and includes the sambhogakaya and the nirmanakaya. When we talk about four kayas, the fourth is the *svabhavikakaya*. This is in fact the union of the three kayas, the fourth being mentioned in order to emphasize their inseparability, their union, and to show that we are speaking of three different aspects of the same buddha.

As Milarepa indicates in the text quoted above, we can discover the three kayas within ourselves by looking directly at the nature of mind. But maybe we should first define the kayas of a buddha.

The Dharmakaya

The dharmakaya is the real buddha. In order to expand this statement, Gampopa quotes the *Prajnaparamita Sutra in Eight Thousand Verses*: "Do not view the tathagata as the form body; the tathagata is the dharmakaya."

If we see without obscuration the dharmakaya within ourselves, we achieve enlightenment and are perfectly purified and liberated. The experiences, the realizations, the state of an arhat, and the phases of the bodhisattva path are just a matter of seeing the dharmakaya more and more clearly. When we've completely realized it, without any obstruction, we've become buddhas. But what is it? The dharmakaya is not "something." Gampopa defines it as follows: "The term 'dharmakaya' simply means the exhaustion of all error—the disappearance of what is of a delusional nature—once the meaning of voidness, the dharmadhatu, has been realized." *Dharmakaya* is only a word that means that all confusion, delusions, and obscurations have disappeared. That's all. It's not something that we get nor something that we see. Until now we have spoken of "seeing" the dharmakaya, but in fact there's nothing to see. Gampopa explains:

> In real essence there is nothing of it whatsoever that really exists—neither as dharmakaya nor as characteristic properties of dharmakaya nor as anything that could serve as a basis for properties (of dharmakaya). Since it is like that, that is how my guru Milarepa explained it.

Therefore, there is nothing to say about it in a way. Nevertheless, eight characteristics are mentioned, not because there's "something," but only because if we talk about it, our human minds need a clear and systematic description in order to understand what is being referred to. These eight characteristics are given in logical order, one leading to the next.

1. *Equal* or *equanimity*. The dharmakaya is the same for all the buddhas and for all beings. It has no ups and downs, no highs or lows, and there's nothing to lose or gain.

2. *Deep, profound*, because the dharmakaya is beyond all concepts, all statements, and all quantitative approaches. It's so difficult to understand because it can't be measured or defined.

3. *Permanent*. Why refer to permanence when until now we've explained that nothing is permanent? We define the dharmakaya as permanent in order to understand that it's neither impermanent nor compounded; that it has no beginning and no end. Actually, it's

beyond both permanence and impermanence, which are just labels that enable us to understand our relative world in a relative way. As the dharmakaya has no substance and can't change, we have to describe it as permanent, but in this context "permanent" indicates an unborn nature that is not compounded and does not relate to a solid entity that exists in and of itself.

Many debates revolve around these definitions. There's a Tibetan saying that goes, "If two philosophers agree, then one of them is not a philosopher, but if two saints do not agree, then one of them is not a saint."

There are many philosophical schools within Buddhism, but all agree on one point: they all share the same final understanding of dharmakaya. Where they diverge is in how they express this understanding. Chandragomin and Chandrakirti, who never doubted each other's realization, were opposed for twelve years in a famous debate that dealt only with these forms of expression, rather than their final meaning.

Some believe that the dharmakaya shouldn't be described as permanent because people could take this the wrong way and think that "permanent" implies the existence of something that is solid, unchanging, and really there, like the *atman*. Others argue that if we don't use this term, people would then deduce that the dharmakaya is impermanent, which is incorrect. It would wrongly imply that the dharmakaya is by nature compounded. All the debates focus on ways of describing the dharmakaya so as to avoid as many misunderstandings as possible. As soon as one philosopher puts forward a description, another will remark, "This will be misinterpreted, so we must therefore describe it this way." Then a third philosopher considers that another formulation would be more appropriate, and so on. This is the case for all philosophical problems.

4. *Homogenous, one.* Here also we assert the opposite of what has been developed previously, namely that nothing is made up of only one thing. As the dharmakaya is not made up of anything and can't be di-

vided, it can only be defined as "one thing," which doesn't mean, however, that it is "something." This simply explains the fact that the dharmakaya can't be divided up into different parts.

5. *Right, totally accomplished,* or *authentic.* The dharmakaya can't form the basis of any concept and nothing can be taken away from it. It is as it is and is perfectly complete within itself.

6. *Pure.* It's stainless, without tarnish or obscuration.

7. *Lucid clarity.* It's free of thought and concept. Therefore dharmakaya is a very clear and luminous consciousness.

8. The last characteristic of the dharmakaya is that it is the basis and foundation for the sambhogakaya.

Graphic representations of the dharmakaya are always dark blue because it's a color that remains unchanged when other colors are added to it. It symbolizes its immutability. Blue is also the color of the sky, a limitless and unobstructed space. This in turn symbolizes its vastness.

The Sambhogakaya

The sambhogakaya is also described as having eight characteristics:

1. The entourage with which it is spontaneously experienced is composed solely of bodhisattvas abiding in the tenth bodhisattva level.
2. The domain in which it is experienced is that of the utterly pure buddhafields.
3. The way that it is experienced is in the form of illustrious Vairochana, and so on.
4. The marks with which it is physically endowed are the thirty-two marks of excellence and the eighty adornments.
5. The Dharma through which it is perfectly experienced is uniquely that of the Mahayana.
6. The enlightened activity that forms its deeds is to predict (the future enlightenment) of the bodhisattvas.

7. Those deeds and so forth are all accomplished without any effort, occurring spontaneously as in the example of the supreme gems (wish-fulfilling gems).
8. Even though it manifests various sorts of form, they are not its true nature; they are like the colors picked up in a crystal.

The sambhogakaya is the manifestation of the clarity that is part of the dharmakaya. When one has a complete understanding, a complete realization of the dharmakaya, from one's point of view, there's nothing that isn't pure and enjoyable. When sambhogakaya forms are represented, they're always youthful and very beautiful, adorned with jewels and ornaments. They express complete enjoyment and represent the pure vision of a buddha. Everything is seen from this point of view when we perceive our true nature, the dharmakaya: nothing is impure and we see all beings as perfect. A buddha perceives other beings as pure, while realizing that they don't see themselves as such.

The Nirmanakaya

The nirmanakaya is the form through which beings perceive a buddha, whose only aim is to help them. This form can manifest through any aspect: as a man, a woman, an animal, a god, music, a bridge, food for the hungry, medicine for the sick, and so on—anything that can be useful to beings.

The nirmanakaya also has eight principal characteristics. Once again I will quote Gampopa:

1. Its basis is the dharmakaya (from which it emanates), without there being any shift.
2. It arises from tremendous compassion, which aspires to benefit every single being.
3. Its domain embraces both the very pure lands and quite impure ones.
4. It endures, without interruption, for as long as the world endures.
5. Its character is to manifest forms as the three types of emanations:

    a. Creative emanations, which are beneficial creations such as great works of art, music, medicine, food, as well as those people endowed with outstanding skills who bring a great deal of benefit to beings;

    b. Birth emanations, which take birth in various bodies in specific types of existences, for example, as a hare; and

    c. Supreme emanations, who manifest the twelve deeds: descent from Tushita heaven, entering the mother's womb, and so forth, and eventually entering great peace.

6. The nirmanakaya makes ordinary worldly beings long for and work toward whichever of the three types of nirvana corresponds to their mentality.

7. The nirmanakaya brings to full spiritual maturity those who are already engaged in the path.

8. The nirmanakaya frees from the fetters of existence those who have reached a full maturity in virtue.

Manifestation of the Three Kayas

The sambhogakaya and the nirmanakaya are form bodies that don't appear without cause. They appear for three reasons.

The first of these causes is the natural power of the blessing that emanates from the dharmakaya. The very nature of the dharmakaya is such that it has the capacity to manifest spontaneously in perceptible forms.

The second cause is the pure view of the beings who can perceive the two form kayas. They've purified the obscurations that prevented them from seeing them.

The vows formulated by the buddhas at the moment they committed themselves to the bodhisattva path are the third cause. They formulated the wish to help beings, and this aspiration created the conditions that enable the buddha emanations to be perceived.

These three conditions have to come together, and one therefore sees how, even at the level of buddhahood, everything is interdependent.

Indeed, if all that was required were the blessings of the buddhas, we would be able to perceive the sambhogakaya and the nirmanakaya at all times. It's the very vow of the buddhas to help beings. They have all the qualities to do so and their powers are limitless; therefore, there shouldn't be any limitation to their capacity to show themselves to beings. However, it's clear that all beings aren't able to perceive them.

If all that we needed were a pure mind, then the presence of the buddhas wouldn't be necessary. In addition, we would see buddhas everywhere, even where they are not. The perception of their forms would in this case only be a hallucination!

Finally, if the buddhas had only to pray in order to be seen, all beings would be able to detect their form since the buddhas are totally impartial and by no means favor some rather than others. However, again, we see that only a small number of beings are able to see them.

We notice therefore that even the buddhas aren't all-powerful, and that at their level also, interdependence is at play. Even buddhas don't have the power to disregard interdependence. We can't blame evil and unfortunate conditions on the buddhas' inactivity because they can find themselves prevented from doing what they would wish, or what would be necessary at that precise moment, if opposing causes and conditions have come together.

I've dealt briefly with the physical attributes of buddhahood. I've also emphasized that it's possible for all beings to attain buddhahood in a single lifetime. Will our physical features therefore change accordingly, and will we be able to observe our spiritual progress in a mirror? In fact, we need to distinguish between two different cases. There's a slight difference between becoming a buddha and being like Buddha Shakyamuni. The latter had the activity, teachings, and physical features of a buddha, and they were perceived by all as such. The form of Buddha Shakyamuni is what we call a form of Supreme Nirmanakaya, the manifestation of which depends on a great number of circumstances and requires what we call the "purification of a buddhafield." When a buddhafield is purified, a buddha appears with all the physical signs that characterize it.

In the Vajrayana, when we talk of becoming a buddha in a single lifetime, we're talking about the individual who becomes a buddha. From this person's own point of view, he or she has no more problems. From that moment on, he or she has all the qualities of a buddha, but these may not necessarily be apparent to everyone. The person doesn't necessarily grow a protuberance and walk around with a halo around his or her head.

It must be emphasized that, although we speak in the Vajrayana of the possibility of achieving buddhahood in a single lifetime, few people actually succeed in doing this. Most reach that state at the moment of death. They recognize the *dharmata* when it manifests and thus attain liberation and enlightenment. This is considered to be reaching enlightenment in this lifetime, as one hasn't yet reached the next. Others attain enlightenment in the bardo state. My own teacher explained to me that it's very difficult to attain enlightenment in this life because our bodies and our environment hinder us.

6. THE ACTIVITIES
OF A BUDDHA

The three kayas aren't something that we obtain thanks to our practice. They don't appear from somewhere else when we become a buddha; they're already present within us right now. We're simply not aware of them. We must remove the veils, the wrappings we've covered them with. From that point of view, our minds can be introduced to the three kayas right now, and such an introduction constitutes the deepest and most direct teaching we can receive. It's what we call Dzogchen, Lamdre, or Mahamudra. The aim of such teachings is to directly introduce the mind to the three kayas, that is to say, to its true nature, buddhahood. Although in a way this is very simple—looking at our mind when it is clear and calm, and seeing its true nature—in reality this is very difficult for the four reasons already mentioned: it's too simple, too close, too good, and too deep. The third Karmapa wrote a text on how to realize the three kayas, and it's about four big volumes! Even if a master tries to introduce his students' minds to it, that doesn't necessarily happen. When someone who has some little experience of it speaks about it, it is very unlikely that the audience will be able to grasp the concept from the outset. Most often, they don't understand what he's talking about and get nothing out of it. This is why there are preliminaries: the students must gradually prepare for it, deepening their understanding little by little.

When our mind becomes calm and clear, we can really look at the ordinary mind, the basic mind, and come to realize that there's actually . . . nothing to see! There is consciousness, but there's nothing anywhere that would have a beginning or an end, a shape, a color, or a substance. It's the unborn nature, unidentifiable, intangible, ungraspable. That's the dharmakaya aspect of the mind.

Although it's ungraspable and without any point of reference, there's nevertheless a clarity, a luminosity, a kind of energy. This is the sambhogakaya aspect of the mind.

At the same time, there are continuous manifestations. Thoughts and emotions constantly arise, coming and going in the mind without interruption: this is the nirmanakaya aspect of the mind.

When we gain a real understanding, a deep realization of this, we're then able to see the three kayas within ourselves at this very moment. They're not something external to us that we should generate: it's simply there. The greater our confidence on this subject, the more realized we are. Seen from this angle, becoming a buddha isn't something far away or too difficult to achieve. All we need to know is how to do it.

There are no more limits for a truly enlightened buddha who has developed wisdom and compassion to the highest level. For the time being, we are limited. We've limited ourselves and others to small things. This is why we encounter so many problems. We differentiate between things "out there" and "in here," between what we like and what we dislike. In this way, we're constantly trapped in problematic situations, in conflicts and disharmony. Because this limited way of seeing things is our only horizon, we suffer and become the source of our own problems. When we open up and break these limits, situations no longer appear as before. We don't become a different person, but we see things in a different way. Our actions are no longer "reactions" but direct actions. This is what buddhahood means.

How can a buddha, a nonconceptual and nondualistic being, help others? Many people wonder how buddhas can help other beings when, from their own point of view, they see all things as pure and don't feel any separateness from beings. Can they perceive and understand the suffering of beings and the need to help them? Saying that buddhas see things in a nonconceptual and nondualistic manner doesn't mean they're unable to perceive the suffering of others. We could compare a buddha to an adult watching children playing. A child builds a sand castle and cries when another destroys it. The adult knows it's no big deal but also knows that the child who's crying is really suffering.

A buddha acts in a spontaneous way without any preestablished plan. He doesn't think, "Yesterday I helped this person, I think that's enough. Today I will help someone else." A buddha's body, speech, and mind all function in a nonconceptual, spontaneous way.

Gampopa gives various examples to illustrate such spontaneous actions. They are very much connected with Indian mythology.

The first example shows the way the body of a buddha appears. Indra, the king of the gods, sits in a palace of lapis lazuli, radiant with light. The beams of light reflect Indra throughout space, and these reflections are sometimes perceived by other beings, who, on seeing them, exclaim, "What an extraordinary king! I wish I could become like him!" Inspired by this vision, they try to behave in a positive manner and help others. Indra himself doesn't know that his image is reflected, where these reflections go, or how they help other beings. In the same way, the appropriate nirmanakaya form of a buddha appears for the sake of the beings who need it where and when the necessary interdependent conditions come together. It naturally emanates from his natural compassion and the power of his previous prayers. A buddha appears where its help is needed, without even making a deliberate decision to do so.

A buddha's speech manifests in the same way. The form emanations and teachings are present everywhere. What we call the treasures of Dharma reflect this principle. The teachings of the buddhas can be heard in the sounds of nature—in the wind, the rustle of the leaves, or the crashing of the waves. They're present everywhere, in the midst of all manifestations. This is what we call the symbolic guru of the universe, which means that whatever we see and experience can become a source of teachings and enlightenment. It isn't a way of seeing things or a subjective projection. The manifestations of buddhas and realized beings can take any form, and these forms don't necessarily need to be alive. They could be music, a hospital, a bridge, a boat, food, water, or anything beings may need.

The body, speech, and mind of a buddha are spontaneous, uncontrolled, limitless, and nonconceptual.

The following examples illustrate how a buddha's mind functions. The first example is that of a cloud. Clouds come and go, and when the right conditions are present, they shed their rain. This rain helps the flowers, trees, and fruits to grow. The clouds don't decide when or where to shed their rain. It just happens. The activities of a buddha happen in the same way.

The second example is that of Brahma, a Hindu god. In Hindu mythology, there are three main deities: one to create the universe, one to preserve it, and a third to destroy it. Brahma is the creator. He can simultaneously take any form that he wishes when necessary. He doesn't have to plan, to run here and there, busy with many things to do, and he doesn't have to worry that he will have no time to do all that has to be done. All the necessary things just happen simultaneously.

The third example is that of the sun. The sun shines constantly and everywhere. It doesn't think that it will shine in one place more than another. Whoever wants to bathe in the sun can just do so without first having to ask for the sun's permission or pay a tax to benefit from a few of its rays. In the same way, the wisdom and compassion of a buddha embraces all beings without bias. The only thing necessary is to open ourselves in order to receive it. Someone who is sitting in a cave under the ground won't receive any warmth or light from the sun. One has to get outside into the sunshine.

The fourth example, the wish-fulfilling gem, is also drawn from Hindu mythology. This jewel that grants all wishes is a bluish stone that must be found somewhere beyond the oceans. Once we have managed to get it, we must wash it with seawater and then with sweet water, wipe it with silk cloths of various colors, and fix it on top of a mast. All we have to do then is pray, and, through the power of the gem, all our wishes will come true. A wish-fulfilling gem doesn't decide to grant this and not that, to help a nice person but refuse to grant the wishes of a nasty person. Whoever follows the right steps gets what he or she prayed for. The blessings and manifestations of a buddha happen in the same way, whenever somebody has created the right situation. When the interdependent circumstances are there, the wish is granted and nothing can stop it.

These different examples all illustrate the spontaneous, unplanned activities of a buddha. There's no judgment, no discrimination, no hold. They happen wherever and whenever the necessary conditions are fulfilled. The activities of a buddha are spontaneous actions and not reactions.

CONCLUSION

I'd like to make a last remark regarding the practice: developing compassion is more a question of understanding than of techniques. I've repeated this all along, but I still wish to stress this important point: to get an intellectual understanding of what we're talking about is relatively simple, but to integrate this understanding at a deeper level is much more difficult. A purely intellectual understanding remains superficial and won't help us when we'll most need it. When integration has taken place, our confidence is strong and stable and our proficiency in the practice increases.

When we listen to teachings, we often think we've understood everything, but it's a completely different matter once we try to put them into practice at home. We discover that they're not an integral part of us, that we haven't completely absorbed them yet. The Tibetans say that the journey from the head to the heart is the longest, and I think that's true. The essence of a real practice is to bring our intellectual understanding to the level of our heart, so as to feel it, to live it. When we understand deeply, the right attitude, the right words, the right action come to us spontaneously, effortlessly. And when we're confident, we act with joy and enthusiasm.

First, try to truly understand the notions taught, and then meditate on them to deepen your understanding. Apply continuously what you've learned in your daily life, but don't get rigid or tense. Certain people tend to take things too seriously, feeling guilty, for example, if they get up late one day for their morning meditation. That's excessive. Your practice shouldn't become a burden, although you should try to maintain a certain regularity. In fact, only this regularity will allow you to stabilize the understanding you have acquired and to use it to cope with the situations of your daily life. When you can practice, rejoice, but if for some reason you can't, there's no need to feel guilty or depressed. Don't turn your practice into a source of stress or worry. You haven't been able to do anything for a few days? That's no disaster. Remember the time when you did nothing at all! To do a little is better than doing nothing at all. Don't take things too seriously, put them in a more realistic perspective.

This last bit of advice ends my commentary on *The Jewel Ornament of Liberation*, Gampopa's most important work. It's not mentioned in the translation but this book came to be because Gampopa was asked to compose it by one of his monks, Dharmashag. Gampopa agreed and dictated the text. This book was thus actually written down by Dharmashag.

I received this teaching from my teacher, Khenpo Lama Rinchen, who received it from Jamgön Kongtrul of Shechen (1901–1960), who in turn received it from Khenpo Tashi Özer (1830–?), who received it from Jamgön Kongtrul the Great (1813–1899).

I'm conscious of not having taught it correctly or as systematically as it should have been taught. In the traditional manner, this text is the subject of a whole year of intensive study. However, the reader should keep in mind that we were limited by time. I've also taken into account that for certain persons in the audience, a lot of this was completely new. I didn't want to bore my audience with a very detailed or academic approach, and I did all I could to make this teaching clear and vivid by using quotes from the great teachers and illustrations from Tibetan folk tales, my own personal experiences, and those of my Western students. I hope I've succeeded, but I ask you to consider this commentary not as a complete and definitive explanation but more as an introduction that may prepare you for a deeper personal study.

DEDICATION OF MERIT

Through the wholesomeness of these good actions,
May all negative emotions and the veils that obscure the mind be
    eliminated,
And may all sentient beings be liberated from the ocean of existence
Stirred by the waves of birth, aging, sickness, and death.

NOTES

FOREWORD

1. Shabkar, *Autobiography of a Tibetan Yogi* (Paris: Albin Michel, 1998).

INTRODUCTION

1. *Dvag po thar rgyan.*
2. The *Dagpo Tarjen* was first translated into English by Herbert V. Guenther under the title *The Jewel Ornament of Liberation* (Berkeley: Shambhala, 1971). It was subsequently translated by Ken and Katia Holmes as *Gems of Dharma, Jewels of Freedom* (Forres, Scotland: Altea Publishing, 1995). A third translation, by Khenpo Konchog Gyaltsen Rinpoche, has been published under the original title, *The Jewel Ornament of Liberation* (Ithaca, N.Y.: Snow Lion Publications, 1998).
3. The Kagyu or Kagyupa (*bka' brgyud pa*) is one of the four main schools of

Tibetan Buddhism. The other three are Nyingma (*rnying ma*), Gelug (*dge lugs*), and Sakya (*sa skya*).

4. The Kadampa (*bka' gdams pa*) tradition traces its origin to the Mahayana (Great Vehicle) teachings of Atisha from the lineage of Nagarjuna and Asanga. It no longer exists as a separate tradition but has been incorporated into the four major contemporary schools of Tibetan Buddhism.

5. The yogic experiential tradition from the lineage of the Indian panditas Tilopa and Naropa and from them to Marpa and Milarepa. Mahamudra (literally, "great seal") is the highest teaching of the Kagyu tradition.

6. A geshe (*dge bshes*) is a scholar with a profound knowledge of the sutras and the Buddhist teachings.

7. Central Tibet.

8. A fuller account of Gampopa's meeting and relationship with Milarepa can be found in Garma C. C. Chang, trans., *The Hundred Thousand Songs of Milarepa* (New Hyde Park: University Books, 1962). See also Jampa Mackenzie Stewart, *The Life of Gampopa* (Ithaca, N.Y.: Snow Lion Publications, 1995).

9. Manjushri was one of the eight close disciples of Buddha Shakyamuni. In Mahayana Buddhism, Manjushri is the bodhisattva who incarnates wisdom.

10. *Dharma* is a Sanskrit word. The Tibetan term is *chö* (*chos*). It has many meanings. Here it means "teaching" or "path." When Buddhists refer to "the Dharma" they are usually referring to the body of teachings leading to enlightenment given by Shakyamuni Buddha and other enlightened beings.

11. The Tibetan words in the text are literally translated as "sons" and "fathers." They refer equally to children or parents.

12. *Lama* is the Tibetan term for teacher, equivalent to the Sanskrit *guru*.

13. *tsawe lama* (*rtsa ba'i bla ma*).

14. *'khrul ba*.

15. The six realms are divided into three upper realms—gods, *asuras* (jealous gods), and humans—and three lower realms—animals, hungry ghosts, and hell beings.

16. *ma rig pa*.

1. THE CAUSE: BUDDHA NATURE

1. *rgyu* (Skt. *hetu*): the cause, which refers to our buddha nature.
2. *Ting nge 'dzin rgyalpo'i mdo.* This is one of the main Mahayana sutras and the one in which the coming of Gampopa is predicted.
3. Skt. *sugatagarbha*; Tib. *bde gshegs snying po.* (*bde gshegs* means "one who entered on the right path"; *snying po* means "the seed" or "the essence").
4. *rigs.*
5. *rigs ched.*

2. THE BASIS: A PRECIOUS HUMAN LIFE

1. *rten:* the basis, which refers to our human birth.
2. *mi lus rin chen.*

3. THE CONDITION: THE SPIRITUAL FRIEND

1. *rkyen* (Skt. *pratyaya*): the favorable condition, which refers to a spiritual friend.
2. *gewe shenyen* (*dge ba'i bshes nyan*). *Gewe* means "virtue" or "positive qualities," and *shenyen* means "friend." We may translate this as "spiritual friend," even if in Tibetan the word "spiritual" is only implied. Ken Holmes translates this term as "good mentor" and explains his choice thus: "The Tibetan term dge ba'i bshes nyan is very evocative, meaning 'friend and relative in virtue.' It gives feelings of closeness, goodness and guidance in something noble, of one with whom there exists a profound link (hence 'relative'). This has sometimes been translated as 'spiritual friend,' a good term but one which can be—and has been—misunderstood. That's why I prefer the word 'mentor,' which means experienced and trusted adviser (OED)." See Ken Holmes and Katia Holmes, *Gems of Dharma, Jewels of Freedom* (Forres, Scotland: Altea Publishing, 1995).
3. *Prajnaparamitasamcayagatha.*
4. *Astasahasrikaprajnaparamita* (*Prajnaparamita in Eight Thousand Verses*).
5. The Three Jewels are the Buddha, the Dharma, and the Sangha, in which a Buddhist takes refuge. See chapter 4 for a detailed explanation.
6. Sangha (Skt.): community of Dharma practitioners.
7. The nirmanakaya, sambhogakaya, and dharmakaya are explained in detail in chapter 5.
8. *byang sa*; Skt. *bodhisattvabhumi.*
9. As he may not have teaching abilities.

4. THE METHOD: THE INSTRUCTIONS OF THE SPIRITUAL FRIEND

1. *bardo:* interval, intermediate time. The *bardo* of death is the period during which the psychophysical elements that constitute the individual progressively dissolve.
2. Skt. *samskara duhkhata.*
3. Skt. *viprinama duhkhata.*
4. Skt. *duhkhata duhkhata.*
5. First level of the bodhisattva path.
6. *bag chags;* Skt. *vasana.*
7. *mdo sde las brgya pa;* Skt. *Karmasatakasutra.*
8. Sukhavati or Dewachen (*bde ba can*): the pure land or "paradise" of Buddha Amitabha.
9. *sems pa'i las.*
10. *bsam pa'i las.*
11. Samadhi: profound meditation; Tib. *ting nge 'dzin.*
12. *jampa* (*byams pa*); Skt. *maitri.*
13. The Middle Way, one of the philosophical schools of Mahayana Buddhism.
14. *Ratnavali.*
15. *nying je* (*snying rje*); Skt. *karuna.*
16. *Tathagatacintyaguhyanirde.*
17. *Abhisamayalankara;* Tib. *Mngon rtogs rgyan.*
18. *tön dam chang chup sem* (*don dam byang chub sems*); Skt. *paramartha bodhicitta.*
19. *kun dzob chang chup sem* (*kun rdzob byang chub sems*); Skt. *samvrti bodhicitta.*
20. The Vinaya is one of the three "baskets" or sections of the Tripitaka, the canon of Buddhist scriptures. The Vinaya is a compilation of the rules of conduct established by the Buddha. There are specific rules for monks, nuns, and lay people.
21. *Rgyu bla ma, The Sublime Continuum,* one of the five treatises of Asanga, whose content was transmitted to him by the Buddha Maitreya.
22. In certain texts two kayas are mentioned, the dharmakaya and the rupakaya. In other texts, four kayas are mentioned, and in the Tantrayana five. But in the majority of the Mahayana texts, three are mentioned.
23. That is to say, gods, divinities, local spirits, elemental forces, and so on.

24. The word for "Buddhist" in Tibetan is *nang pa,* meaning "interior," one who turns one's gaze inward.

25. *drup tap (sgrub thabs),* the method of accomplishment, the text of a practice that aims at the experience of ultimate reality through meditation. It includes a whole system of visualizations, recitations, rituals, and meditations, centered around a deity or a cycle of deities.

26. A *mala* is a 108-bead rosary used to count the recitation of mantras or prayers.

27. *tsultrim (tshul khrims);* Skt. *shila.*

28. *samten (bsam gtan);* Skt. *dhyana.*

29. *sherab (shes rab);* Skt. *prajna.*

30. *Para* means "the other side" and *mita* "to go beyond."

31. *jinpa (sbyin pas);* Skt. *dana.*

32. The difference between *yeshe (yes shes)* and *sherab (shes rab)* is subtle. *She* means "knowledge," and *rab* means "best, superior." *Sherab* therefore means "the best knowledge." *Yeshe* means "the knowedge that is true from the beginning," pristine, primordial, fundamental wisdom. When our sherab is completely developed, one speaks of *yeshe.*

33. *tsultrim;* Skt. *shila.*

34. These are the rules followed by monks and nuns.

35. *zöpa (bzod pa);* Skt. *kshanti.*

36. *shinay (shi gnas).*

37. *lagtong (lhag mthong).*

38. A *siddha* is an accomplished yogi.

39. *rten 'brel yan lag bcu gnyis* (Skt. *pratitiya samutpada*): the twelve links of interdependent production: (1) Ignorance (*avidya*); (2) Volition (*samskara*); (3) Conscience (*vijnana*); (4) Name and Form (*namarupa*); (5) Sense Faculties (*ayatanam*); (6) Contact (*sparsha*); (7) Sensation (*vedana*); (8) Desire or Thirst (*trshna*); (9) Grasping (*upadanam*); (10) Becoming (*bhava*); (11) Birth (*jati*); (12) Aging and Death (*jara maranam*).

40. The levels and stages of meditation mentioned here should not be confused with the "forms" of meditation, namely, *shamatha* and *vipashyana.*

41. *sherab;* Skt. *prajnaparamita.*

42. *Prajnaparamitasamcayagâtha.*

43. *Akshayamatipariprcchasûtra.*

44. *Pramânavaritkâ;* Tib. *Rnam 'grel.*

45. Skt. *mâra:* demon.

46. *Anavataptanâgarâjapariprcchâsûtra.*

INDEX